OSSIE CLARK

The Highs and Lows of a Legendary Fashion Designer

Tommy Kennedy IV

NEW HAVEN PUBLISHING LTD

Published 2023
First Edition
NEW HAVEN PUBLISHING LTD
www.newhavenpublishingltd.com
newhavenpublishing@gmail.com

All Rights Reserved
The rights of Tommy Kennedy IV, as the author of this work, have been asserted in accordance with the Copyrights, Designs and Patents Act 1988.
No part of this book may be re-printed or reproduced or utilized in any form or by any electronic, mechanical or other means, now unknown or hereafter invented, including photocopying, and recording, or in any information storage or retrieval system, without the written permission of the
Authors and Publisher.

Cover Design © Alan Blizzard

Copyright © 2023 Tommy Kennedy IV
All rights reserved
ISBN: 978-1-912587-81-0

Preface

It's essential to let you know I never knew Ossie Clark. I saw him once in my lifetime, which doesn't count as much. But, as a schoolchild, I still remember his visit and the impact he had on me. Ossie Clark brought us extraordinary creations. Before he died at 54 years old, fashion design was his gift. Anybody alive in the 60s and 70s with the remotest interest in style would know him as a man who underwent many transformations.

I felt predestined to author this book about an extraordinary man who had such energy and vitality in his prime. Since last year, I have met many people who knew Ossie. I went to a friend's funeral in Notting Hill, where I met Middlesborough Barry, an outrageous and glitzy costume designer who lived in Notting Hill for over 40 years. He asked me, "Hey, what are ya doing these days, Tommy?" as he fluttered his eyelids and broke into laughter. I replied that I was about to draft a book about Ossie Clark, and he said, "Aye, Tommy lad, you must come to my house. I knew Ossie and have his diaries to help with ya research."

I couldn't believe it. A few days later, I went to Barry's flat, climbed the stairs and rapped on the door. He opened the entrance with a flourish and said, "Welcome to my humble home." I stepped into his room and discovered a treasure trove of paintings, vinyl records and books. Barry handed over a well-thumbed copy of *The Ossie Clark Diaries* and reminisced about Ossie. He told me his friends wanted to get him and Ossie together. He said nobody liked Diego Cogalato. They found him creepy. "I couldn't understand what Ossie saw in him," he added.

I listened till he had finished. I thanked him. He led me to the door; I rushed down the stairs and took the book home. I couldn't wait to start the journey of discovering Ossie and his life. Throughout the weeks, I re-read it cover to cover. It amazed me what I learned about Ossie's life. It was brutal and honest, almost to the point that I felt like a voyeur in his life.

The position he holds in people's memories is remarkable. He stands up with the most fabulous designers of the 20th century. The French have Yves Saint Laurent; the Italians have Gianni Versace. In authoring this book, I will try to bring Ossie alive during his growing up and his turbulent adult life. I have found him to be a man of great warmth and wit who helped many on his rise to the pinnacle of the fashion world. In addition, he had an insatiable curiosity about life and the history of style. On the other hand, he was afflicted with depression and an explosive temper throughout his life, shocking many. When his star began to fade in the mid-70s, his life wasn't over. He lived a further 20 years and still chased his dreams and stimulated his friends around him. Yet, 26 years after his demise, he is still an enigma, loved by his family and abandoned by many of the celebrities he clothed.

I want to dig deeper into the man himself. Of course, I don't know about the entirety of his life. Anybody who writes a biography is crazy or obsessive. I'm a bit of both as I grind my teeth and scratch my head. I wonder what I can bring to the table in writing about Ossie's life. After months of research, I will try to understand what made him tick. We must realise he was very different from the usual run-of-the-mill character we meet on life's journey. I feel confident there will be fashion purists who won't be satisfied or will want to see more photographs. Still, if you want to see these photos, there are umpteen all over the internet to satisfy your curiosity. Ossie was an outsider. He came to London from a different world. My northern background influences my writing style, and I have some idea of what Ossie went through.

Ossie sprang from good working-class stock with spirit and aspirations. He didn't drop lucky; he initially worked his butt off to get to where he did in his career. He wasn't part of the elite of London, but he soon made his presence sensed. He wasn't an arse licker. He came to the counter of the rich and famous with his talent and provided women with newfound confidence. It brought him into contact with people with money and the good sense to buy into what he made; these weren't cheap, throwaway garments. I make no apologies for him. He left many friends and family in awe of his talent and they loved him with all his faults. Many still remember him today, and his name is tantamount to style in the fashion world.

In my re-creation of Ossie's life, I have read and interviewed his friends to get to know him. I haven't put questions to his family. Their thoughts are their own, and I'm sure written somewhere. This will be a picture of the man and the world around him. I want to bring the era to life, so I must mention what happened around these times to the younger readers who may not know about Ossie and his generation. This is a man with whom I feel lucky to spend time on, recalling his life, warts and all. My purpose is not to offend anybody. I hope to do Ossie's memory justice and stimulate some working-class kids somewhere to achieve their dreams with demanding work and self-belief.

His faithful friends, the people who weren't famous, have said good things about him, although, without a doubt, Ossie had his imperfections - can any of us claim we haven't?

To appreciate Ossie, we must not define him by the clothes he designed; although it is poignant to think he is still remembered, there was so much more to the man than this. His family were proud of his triumphs as a loving father, friend and son. I want to take the reader on a voyage of discovery and map out his life from a modest background in the north of England and the heights he soared.

He remained his genuine, frank, authentic self, and some people may have found him hard to take with his abrasive attitude. However, at least you knew where you stood with him. If he thought you deserved it, he would speak his mind. He never pretended to be somebody he wasn't. He was a rare breed in this life. He despised pretentiousness and would point it out if somebody thought they were better than him. This was forged in his DNA.

I'm sure he could have turned his life around when he was killed. Hence, I have tried to lessen the loss to his friends, and show how one rare, unconventional man from such a warm background, in my hometown of Warrington, achieved the recognition he deserved, and inspired a generation.

Some people look down their noses at failure, but if you don't try, you will never know… and to be honest, who gives a hoot what anybody thinks? Ossie didn't.

Content

Strange Coincidences	7
Beamont Technical School	18
Manchester School of Art	29
London	36
Notting Hill	51
Hippy-Ocrats	64
New York	85
Percy Savage	90
Juno Gemes	93
Rivals	99
On the Dole	111
Barbados	120
Hampstead Heath	130
Tragedy	137
The Sicilian	146
Murder	154
Aftermath	160
Epilogue	167
My Thoughts	174
About the Author	182

Strange Coincidences

I sit in my council flat and I can sense Ossie urging me on; almost as if I am being channelled to write his life story, as crazy as this may seem. I believe he was angry when *The Ossie Clark Diaries* were published because there was so much he would have left out and also added: he wanted to set the record straight. He wasn't miserable all the time. His diaries make for a sad read in parts, but if you figure out between the lines, you can tell a lot of it was said with his tongue firmly in his cheek. For the readers who haven't read them, I would like to bring a smile to their faces when they think of Ossie. I want to get to the heart of the matter and tell this with a sense of humour. I now live five minutes from where he once lived on Penzance Place in Holland Park in the 1990s. I stop and think about this dramatised biography I will embark on. I will endeavour to introduce him in a story-like way, but some of the characters are still alive, and I must be thoughtful of their feelings. Ossie lived an incredible life full of passion and originality. However, even in the latter days of his life, he'd been used to getting by without much money. He still lived in the best part of London, sought after by people with cash, close to the tube station and the exquisite Holland Park with its majestic Japanese gardens. Most people would get down and be thankful to live there.

The area of Clarendon Cross and Holland Park Avenue close by is vibrant. I decide to take a stroll and check where his flat was situated. The smell of flowers and trimmed grass hang in the breeze and the spring sunshine is on my face. I admire the elm tree-lined, expansive, well-kept streets, a short saunter from Notting Hill. It might have been a housing association flat, but Ossie spent many happy years there. The apartment was small, but it was his home. After years of being rootless, and relying on friends and family, nobody could take it away from him after his career turned downward. He would have been one happy man to move in. The newspapers made a great deal out of where he lived, but it didn't do justice to me. It is an affluent area and one of the safest places to live in the capital.

Of course, Simon Cowell, David Beckham and Ed Sheeran live close by in their twenty-million-pound properties across Holland Road. However, as the New York superstar Madonna once said, it doesn't matter where you live in London; you are always within gobbing distance of a council estate. She should know: she owned property here.

Ossie and I were both former pupils of Beamont Technical School in Warrington, from different generations. Ossie went on to art college, to achieve something with his life, and it's been a revelation for me after months of research to learn about his colossal achievements. So, what qualifications do I have to write this story? Well, we came from similar backgrounds. I have been through countless trials, and I can see similarities in his life which resonated with mine. However, the more I delved into his generation, the more it gripped me.

I'd travelled the world, lived high, driven flashy cars, and lived in exotic countries until everything went skew-whiff. I ended up broke and homeless. I had nobody to turn to, and nothing left apart from my sense of humour. Still, I have spirit and have learned more than I have earned in my lifetime. I'm still alive and have come to terms with everything. Life is an adventure with all its kinks and quirks. Whatever happens in your life, keep a sense of comedy about it all.

Moreover, I know Ossie did. This is not a sad tale. Although his life ended in tragedy, Ossie's sense of humour shone through from what I have gathered. Yes, he suffered from depression and endured periods of melancholy, an affliction that can strike at any time in many people's lives. But, as we say in the north, he was a character of the highest order. Now we shall see how his personality developed. I feel privileged to relate his life from an alternative perspective.

Ossie put pen to paper frequently in his diaries. This is my version. I have used my imagination about the dialogue, which is representative and not verbatim. I hope you will stick with me through this journey of revelation.

So come on, let's hang out and see what we can uncover.

On June the 9th, 1942, Britain had been at war for the last two years and ten months. People all over the UK were sure that it would soon be over. In a maternity ward in Liverpool, Ossie's beloved mother, Anne Clark, lay on a bed alert and awake, a gleam of sweat daubed over her brow, eager for the pregnancy to conclude. As the contractions became more robust, she arched her back and prayed all would go well. She couldn't wait to meet the new child.

A pungent antiseptic smell flowed through the air. The floors were spotless; the hospital was packed. Anne's husband, Samuel, hovered outside. He checked his watch for the umpteenth time and paced around, his brow furrowed with expectation, hopeful all would be well. They'd stood around for some time, and it wouldn't be a moment too soon.

Samuel drew his hankie out and wiped his forehead.

By his side stood their 16-year-old daughter, Kay.

She tugged on his sleeve." Dad, don't worry, it will soon be over; you're not pregnant."

He propped his arm on her shoulder and kissed her head. "Let's hope she's here soon, you cheeky madam."

The nurses were rushed off their feet, expectant mothers crammed in together. Anne's body could sense the contractions; her face flushed and tingled, the air palpable with anticipation. The nurse gathered the sheets and plumped up the pillows, trying to make her relax." Don't worry, the baby will soon be here."

"I hope so," Anne replied.

She agonised for seven days in labour; she must have been terrified. When she heard, a few months earlier, that Walton Hospital almost took a bomb through the roof one night, it's a wonder she didn't give birth there and then.

Anne perceived the baby's imminent arrival; she sank back into the mattress and gave one final push. As the midwife probed, she said, "Come on, love, the baby is on the way." The nurse squeezed her hand. Anne could feel the pain with each contraction. Before long, the head of the baby came out with the last pull: a dark-haired boy bawled into the world. His astrological star sign made him a

Gemini. He would inherit all the star's classic qualities: imaginative, witty, talkative, and ironic, with cobalt grey eyes.

After a few minutes, Anne gave a slow movement of the head, incredulity written on her face. Then she composed herself and said, "Thanks, love. I can't believe we've got another boy."

The midwife passed the baby over. Anne reached out, held him close to her chest and checked him over. Her eyes were radiant with pride. The doctor examined the boy and said, "He will do something with those hands. Have you seen the size of them?"

"He's got enormous hands, you say, doctor. He must get them from his father. I hope they will do him some good."

The doctor smiled.

Samuel pushed the doors open and strode into the ward, followed by their daughter. Each looked down at the baby, disbelief stamped on their faces.

With a hesitant smile, in a shaky voice, Samuel said, "Well, I'm stunned, darling. We've got another mouth to feed, and it isn't a girl. So I guess we better repaint the spare room."

Anne's face, although radiant, looked drawn; exhaustion set in. Anne Grace Clark and Samuel Duncan Clark, mother and father, were flabbergasted. They'd decorated the spare room pink for a baby girl.

Kay leaned over, stroked the baby's chin, looked at her mother, and said, "Aw, mam, he's so adorable. He looks so like you."

Anne replied, "Give over. He looks like his father."

Kay smiled." Wait till the rest of the kids see him; our Sammy and John will be made up. They've got a brother. I can't wait to get him home; he will be spoilt. What will we call him?"

Anne thought about it. She was shattered by the pregnancy and couldn't think straight.

"I'm not sure - it's such a shock." Anne gazed at the midwife and said, "Come on, love, you think of a name for him. You've been fantastic throughout the pregnancy. It would be an honour for me."

The midwife smoothed her uniform, mulled it over and said, "Why don't you call him Raymond?

Anne replied," Raymond, it's a lovely name. I'm so overjoyed he is here and healthy; thanks so much for all you've done for me over the last week."

Kay interjected:" Aw, mam, let me hold him."

As she plucked the baby from her mother, her eyes dawdled over his face, and she kissed him, cuddled him, and said, "You are so precious and huggable. Come on, our Raymond, smile."

Her face was full of joy as she placed him back in her mother's arms.

" You looked tired, mam. Dad, come on, let's leave her in peace. We can come back tomorrow." She tended over her mother's bed, stroked her hair, and kissed her forehead. "You have a good sleep tonight, Mam."

"Yes, I'm shattered. You two go home and cook your dad's tea tonight."

They bade her farewell. The nurse took the baby from Anne, who drifted off to sleep. Nine days later, another Scouse legend was born, the exceptional Paul McCartney, who would cross paths with Raymond 25 years later.

The hospital discharged Anne a few days later. Samuel carried their baby home to meet the rest of the children: his eldest sister, Gladys, 18; Beryl, 12; Sammy, 8; and 4-year-old John. They showered him with love from the moment he arrived. He came into a warm and loving family full of characters who knew about life and had great humour. Liverpool is filled with people with these qualities, so it was from this background that the boy would learn about life.

Still, with the war on, the Luftwaffe had tried to flatten the city. It became a prime target for the bombers, and Birkenhead, its twin across the Mersey, was the country's biggest west coast port. Supplies were brought in via Canada and the USA. Britain needed these provisions, and the Germans wanted to halt them.

The port city of Liverpool was a critical target. The seven-night blitz between the 1st and 7th of May 1941 was one of the most intense attacks outside London. It showered death on the citizens below with tons of explosive bombs. It caused immense destruction to the city centre and the nearby port area. This made the family nervous. Still, they did their business; the kids took turns with the pram and pushed Raymond around the streets. They couldn't have been prouder.

Anne loved to draw Raymond close and breastfeed him.

" Coochie coo, you precious little boy."

Her eyes shone with pure love as she gazed at his head and stroked his hair. Then, as he sucked, she caressed his face, strengthening the maternal bond.

The elder children were on hand if she needed help with his nappies or the household chores.

Samuel would peek over the *Liverpool Echo* and watch them when he returned from work, plonked down in his favourite armchair, with the smell of food from the kitchen. Ossie grew up in a happy, tense household throughout the war.

Food rationing made life difficult. Still, it was all part of the war effort. The family got by on the provisions they bought: eight oz of sugar, four oz of bacon, eight oz of cheese, and two oz of tea. Eggs weren't rationed, but it could be hard to find them. The Government cut the milk allowance to three pints a week for each person in 1942, although pregnant women and children were allowed more. It forced people to think about what they ate and how much they wasted. However, people still found things to whine about, and the endless queues to buy food drove them nuts.

Anne would rip coupons from the ration books and hand them to the rest of the family when they wanted food. Their clothes were rationed; each garment required a certain number of coupons. They gave the adults sixty-six coupons a year.

The family got used to the conditions. They also bought on the black market from the local spivs who saw a business opportunity—serving up to the locals. They made an excellent turnover; they could get their hands on women's stockings and luxuries which weren't sold or scarce. Close to the docks, all kinds went through the ports. Luxury goods always seemed to be available at exorbitant prices.

Raymond's parents discussed a move out of Liverpool, to protect their children from the terror campaign raids they'd expected.

Samuel said, "I think it's about time we moved out of the area, for the kids 'sake."

Anne replied, "Yes… let's think it over, but you may be right. Although I love Liverpool, and leaving our friends behind will be a massive wrench." The conversation moved back and forth over the following weeks. However, after further discussions, they concluded that evacuation would be the best route. The family moved to the village of Oswaldtwistle, three miles from Blackburn in East Lancashire, with a small population of under ten thousand. Times were hard for its residents, but they were much safer. The family moved in behind one of the town's local shops, and settled in for the duration of the war.

It was a traumatic few years before Europe's hostilities were declared over on May the 8th, 1945. The news of Germany's surrender touched the rest of the world. Throngs of people congregated on the streets to celebrate. However, the day was poignant for the families who had lost their loved ones through the six years the conflict had raged across Europe.

Three months later, everybody thought the war in the Far East had reached its conclusion; however, when the Americans dropped the atomic bomb on Hiroshima in Japan on the 6th of August 1945, this failed to end the war. A second bomb descended through the skies on Nagasaki on the 9th of August. Finally, at noon on the 15th of August 1945, Emperor Hirohito announced the surrender of Japan.

An estimated 70,000 to 135,000 people died in Hiroshima and 60,000 to 80,000 in Nagasaki. In addition, the nuclear radiation released by the bombs caused thousands more to die in the weeks, months and years ahead.

We should pray we never see an atomic bomb plunge through the skies again.

The family returned to normality over the next four years. However, another move was on the horizon, which made a massive impact. In 1949, when Raymond was aged seven, the family travelled to Longford in the north-west town of Warrington in Lancashire, a couple of miles outside the bustling centre.

They moved into 5 Sandy Lane, a typical semi-detached with a front and back garden. These council houses were built around the country in the 1930s. The house stood close by to where the A49 is now. It was more like the countryside back in those days.

The family soon settled into their new life. It wasn't long before the smells of lovely home cooking circulated throughout the house. The mantelpiece, lined with photographs, became a home for the Clarks.

There weren't many cars on the streets, which allowed the boys to play football outside. The girls engaged in hopscotch, a popular game in the 40s. The teenage girls drew on the ground with chalk, and hopped and skipped in and out of the squares. They would shout with delight if they won. This kept them amused and out of their parents 'way with simple games like hide and seek and marbles.

The men toiled in the local factories: Ryland's, the wire-drawing firm, Longford Wire, and the steelworks Monks Hall. Warrington was an industrial town which embraced the Industrial Revolution in the 18th century and developed. They made the River Mersey navigable, and as a result, the town flourished and became packed with shops and pubs during its expansion and a desirable place to live.

An American airbase in nearby Burtonwood, two miles northwest of Warrington, became the central military installation in Europe after the war. It was like a small town, and the Yanks, as they were known, boosted the area's economy. You would spot the GIs who drove through the town centre, eyeing the local ladies. They fetched glamour to the town. The girls wanted to meet the GIs and dance at the live gigs. Many girls met their future husbands and left Warrington to start a new life in America. The local guys resented the Americans with their money and flash ways.

Also, many women were left behind to rub their pregnant stomachs, unsure where the father went as he flew back to the States, never to return.

The streets were safe though, a perfect place to raise the kids, with schools and churches, and the family established themselves in their new home and made friends. Warrington is in between two major cities, Liverpool and Manchester; each is a short drive away. The 70-mile River Mersey swirls its way through the town.

Not much has been written about Warrington, but Ossie's character was formed in the town. Some unusual people came to the world's attention from this working-class environment. Who would have thought Burt Kwouk, the actor who played Cato in *The Pink Panther*, would have come from here? Actor Pete Postlethwaite and many others come from the town.

When Ossie grew up in the north, the men went to the bookies to gamble a few shillings on the nags and the pubs shut at 2.30pm on a Sunday. Afterwards, everybody would pile home for the Sunday roast. The family took their weekly bath in a grey cast iron one hung up on the scullery wall. Anne would take it down and fill it with hot water from a kettle and pans while each waited their turn, and they used lifebuoy soap to cleanse themselves. No mod cons in those days. The coal man brought the coal and dumped it in the yard. The milkman clinked the milk bottles on the polished red doorstep each day for the morning brew. You wedged a shilling coin in the electric meter under the stairs and heard the metallic clang as it dropped into the coin box below, and turned the key, and the lights switched on.

The council sent a man around each week to collect the rent and woe betide anybody who didn't have the money to pay. Ossie's family weren't wealthy, but they got by.

If you had nowt but your family, you were rich. Ossie was surrounded by his family. A treat in their lives was chips, gravy, or a marvellous piece of battered fish. Who needs champagne and caviar? The simple things in life bring so much pleasure. Of course, life was a lot simpler in those days. Men tended to their allotments or raced pigeons; crown bowls were another popular sport in the town.

The northwest of England is remarkable; the people are sincere and amenable. They will talk with a stranger to make them feel welcome. In those days, the men found work easy to come by, and Raymond's parents throve. All the children picked up the work ethic from their father.

Anne worked at home, with her mother's exceptional talent for knitting. She'd knit jumpers for the kids, and inspired Raymond as he watched her, with pride in his mum's talent.

There are many accents around the regions of the northwest. The kids noticed Raymond's twang, so they dubbed him Ossie after the village of Oswaldtwistle. It stuck for the rest of his life. Warrington is one of the most significant towns in the northwest, surrounded by other towns - Chester, Wigan, Widnes and St Helens, all a bus ride away. The people were sharp and loved a fun time; the place was awash with pubs and clubs. People looked to the future after the war. They wanted to have fun and forget the past.

Warrington's Rugby League team drew tens of thousands of people each Sunday. Ossie treasured his childhood, encircled by his relations of all ages; he learnt his quick wit, love of women, and gossip, which stayed with him. He couldn't have failed to notice the larger-than-life characters he came across in his school days; everybody is a comedian with a tremendous northern sense of humour—however, Warrington, with its reputation for great pubs and clubs scattered all over, was a magnet for the people of the town. When the men returned from a gruelling day, the factory workers would expect a hot meal on the table.

It was a time captured like a dream by the Warrington artist Eric Tucker, who's been touted as the secret Lowry, with the discovery of over 400 paintings and thousands of sketches. He drew on life in the northwest. He believed that the wealthiest life could be found amongst the lowest echelons of society. As with many renowned artists, he didn't become known until after his death in 2018, aged 86.

Although Ossie grew to love ballet, the aroma of flowers, the moon, and the stars, it would be a matter of time before his curiosity would lead him to search for adventure.

There was a keen sense of community. To stand out, you had to be a character. His parents guided Ossie, and he was exposed to music by his father, who played many instruments. In his younger days, he served in the merchant navy as a chief steward and played in jazz bands on the merchant ships between Liverpool and New York. As a result, Ossie was more aware of the world around him than most kids his age.

He was influenced by his elder sister Gladys, 18 years his senior, a seamstress. He would observe and style dresses for dolls. The family proved to be resourceful; this rubbed off on Ossie.

He went to St Oswald's Church with his brother, John, close to Winwick Hospital, the local asylum. They both joined the choir.

Christine Clark, the wife of his brother John, recalls in 2022 how both boys excelled in the choir. Ossie won a medal for singing, and they travelled around over the years to Chester and York cathedrals. She remembers John told her Ossie would sit in the back of the church on the polished wooden pews, sketching. His days were full of exploration. He never sat around. He loved to be outside with friends.

Kay, his sister, had worked in London in a jazz band. Her two children, Carol and Jimmy Melia, became like siblings to Ossie when they moved back from London to spend a few years in Warrington. The girls all moved out and married as the years rolled by.

Ossie was a bright and cheerful child aged seven; he'd been enrolled at St Margaret's Primary Junior School, an old Victorian building with a gravelled grey yard which tutored the local kids from the area. In his final year at junior school, Ossie prepared for the 11-plus exam. When the day arrived, the pupils sat silent as the teachers walked up and down, distributing the test papers to each nervous child.

They knew these exams would dictate their futures and which schools they would be allocated to after the holidays. Anne made sure Ossie did his homework, although, like most boys, he hated it and found it a chore. Still, he persevered and got on with his studies.

There was a 3-tier system back in the 50s, consisting of grammar, technical, and secondary schools. The grammar schools took the brightest kids, who passed the 11-plus exam. The technical school took the most theoretically minded and could train them to be engineers, architects or work supervisors. Lastly, secondary modern kids were the ones with the lowest marks.

Ossie sat at his wooden desk, took the test, and scribbled down his answers; when the teacher told them to put their papers down, the bell rang, and all the kids were glad to get out of there.

" I'm just trying to change the world one sequin at a time."
Lady Gaga

Beamont Technical School

Over the summer holidays, there was the sound of an envelope slipping through the door. Alerted by the noise, Ossie's mother made her way to the front door. She stopped, picked the letter off the carpet, and hurried into the kitchen, expectation written over her face. She'd been looking for this letter. She found her glasses, tore open the envelope, and cast an eye over the official notepaper.

She called out, "Raymond, come into the kitchen." The smell of tea and home-cooked sausages drifted around his nostrils as he entered the room. Anne said, "Well done, son; come here and hug your mother." Ossie wrapped his arms around her; they kissed and embraced. "What happened, Mam? Have the exam results arrived?"

"Yes, son, you've been accepted for Beamont Technical in September."

This delighted Ossie; most of his friends wanted to go there. He didn't make it to the grammar school, but he was glad, as it would have meant a three-mile bus ride to Bottler Grammar every day. So, at the end of the summer holidays, he went to the school on O'Leary Street in Orford in September 1953, a ten-minute stroll from the family home.

On his first day at school, he wore a new uniform: a black blazer with the school crest emblazoned on his breast pocket, and a crisp white shirt with a black and gold striped tie hung from his neck. It's a massive thing in a boy's life to leap from junior to senior school and encounter kids from various schools around the town.

Ossie soon realised the hierarchy at the school. It wasn't uncommon to receive a slap or a punch in the face from the older boys, who bullied the new children if they thought they could get away with it.

Before you went to the senior school, rumours abounded that the older boys would force your head down the toilets on the first day. The kids who arrived would be on their guard for bullies; his older family warned Ossie not to worry and to stand up for himself if anybody tried it on.

The new boys were more interested in sports and playing with friends. Ossie's unusual eye took in all the school's unfamiliar sights and sounds. Like a prisoner on his first day at a prison, checking out how to survive, it could be a scary day for a new arrival.

This wasn't a school where you were treated carefully. You would soon learn anything could happen in the playground. You would learn which boys to avoid because somebody could and would make your life hell if you didn't; some older boys would bully you, and search your pockets for cash and steal your bus fare or dinner money so they could go to the local shop and buy cigarettes. There was almost a look of joy on the older boys' faces as they cast an eye over for the new arrivals who looked like they might have cash. Suppose you looked weak, and wouldn't give any hassle and hand your money over? They would be all over you. All the older boys remembered their first day at school. They knew how a new kid would feel.

And the kids were too scared and intimidated to tell their teachers, who would turn an eye to it all, unless a parent came to the school and said their child was getting bullied. And if they did, the kid would get picked on again when the furore died down a few days later.

Ossie knew all this and acted thus. Although he wasn't a mug, there was no way he wouldn't stand up for himself. He would have felt nervous on his first day at this school run by a shower of bastards who loved to take their petty frustrations out on the pupils, and delighted in humiliating you for no other reason than they could get away with it. The teachers could be ferocious when they lost their tempers.

One boy shouted at Ossie, "Are you a bum boy?" as he strolled by. Ossie laughed and shot back at him with his two fingers. "Piss off, knob-head. Bring your sister around. I will show you if I'm a bum boy or not." This shut the bully down instantly; beating him in an argument was hard. He was sharp as a switchblade and would always have the last word. Ossie was full of quips. From years of experience at home, he'd honed his comebacks. He knew if anybody took the piss, you fired back with your fiery wit.

I remember the stories of the pupils 'ritual embarrassments, which I believe were far worse than when I went there in the 70s. In the 50s, it would have been a nightmare if you were a shy, reserved kid with no confidence to come to school and face the wrath of the teachers. No wonder kids hate school under these conditions. Few would have happy memories of a carefree childhood if they were slapped about so much.

The girls played the game. Some were bitches, though, and picked on some of the other girls in their class. If you were fat, ginger, or wore glasses, your days were numbered because some little bastard would want to degrade you.

It must have made Ossie laugh, though he wasn't one of those boys who would cower in fear. And he knew how to look after himself in any verbal confrontations. The last thing a bully would want is somebody with a sharp tongue and the brains to back it.

So they would move on to the next victim and leave Ossie alone. Ossie had a much easier time at school than many other kids. He mentioned nothing in his diaries, so we can assume it was like water off a duck's back. He was made of much sterner stuff; it didn't take Ossie long to settle in and excel in technical drawing and geometry classes.

Beamont Technical School was a mixed school, with a large assembly hall, surrounded by football pitches and hockey fields. The dining room smelled of school dinners, which were vile. Rugby was the main game for kids; Ossie loved to play football, and rugby, the central team sport, didn't enamour him. Warrington has a rugby league team, with a stadium in Wilderspool causeway, played by the working classes around the north of England; rugby union, played by the public schools down south, has different rules.

Ossie already showed his individuality. He followed nobody and did his own thing with his style and fashion. In addition, he had an excellent knack for Mathematics which would serve him well in the years ahead.

Ossie intimidated some boys because of his way of thinking. But, for sure, he didn't care. He was surrounded by the love of his family, which gave him this inner strength and sense of self-worth. Perhaps with overconfidence, he was fun, making the other kids laugh with his merciless wit.

You dealt with the bullies but learned to cope with the teachers, who could be brutal; you stood up when they entered the room. I'm sure some of them were alcoholics, and you never knew what mood they were in, but you soon found out. The kids were put in line as the teachers carried their canes, ready to beat the youngsters for any infringement.

They would fling books at the kids or, worse, the chalk duster. The pain as it bounced off your head in a cloud of dust was terrible. They'd yank you by your ears and hair and twist till the frightened schoolboy howled out in pain. Their favoured punishment was when they called you out to receive your retribution. It was scary to see Mr Atherton, the metalwork teacher, who stood 6ft tall, a cane in hand, lashing it through the air as a petrified kid approached his desk; thoughts swirling through your brain, shit, this will hurt. With a look of satisfaction, he sprayed spittle and bad breath in your face. "Hold your hand out," he said as he took a jump and thrashed you with six of the best. All the teachers would smack you without hesitation if you stepped out of line.

The women teachers would make you bend over a chair and raise the flap of your blazer so they could get a good shot at your soft buttocks with a small wooden bat, and God did it sting. Nevertheless, you pretended it didn't.

The teachers were so warped that it made you wonder how they got away with their viciousness. Or perhaps this was just my experience. No wonder Ossie developed a strong rebellious mind in this environment. You needed a sharp sense of humour, or the teachers and teenagers would mess with your head if you let the bastards. Unfortunately, this was a harsh atmosphere for a kid to grow up in.

The girls loved it the most if you had a sense of humour. Even if you took the mickey in a good-natured way, you could reel them in, and this is where Ossie came into his own. He knew how to give it out big-time. He learned from an early age how to be sarcastic, and if you gave it out, you would understand you had to take it back. Is it any wonder how Ossie would treat people in later life? No way he would back down in an argument. Working-class kids the country over won't take nonsense. The northern banter is a joy to behold when you get a group of them together; there should be a scriptwriter to record these moments.

Do you know why northern comedians are so funny? This must be their defence mechanism for any situation; if you couldn't make them laugh or put them down with a one-liner, you sure better learn to fight. You had to be always on your lookout. There was no escape from the teachers being given free rein to dish out punishment for any trivial abuse of the rules. If your homework came in late, they would mistreat you in front of the class of sniggering teenagers. Some hard kids were in the ranks, which would only breed resentment. The teachers were bullies at this school. Many kids rebelled against the injustices they met daily in the classroom.

Ossie found his way through the school system. Luckily, he found an ally in the art teacher Mr Thomas, who reeked of paint and cigarettes. This tall, unusual man would lean over and admire Ossie's artwork.

He said, "You should get your mother to enrol you in the art college on a Saturday morning."

Ossie replied, "Thanks, sir. I will mention it to my mam and see what she reckons." When he went home, he talked to his mother as they sat at the formica-covered table in the kitchen.

Anne said, "I'll ask your father and see what he thinks about it. You deserve the chance, son," as she placed his plate of chips and eggs on the table. Ossie devoured the meal, scraped back his chair, and ran outside to play with his mates.

When Samuel returned from work, Anne told him, "The teacher reckons we should enrol our Raymond in the art classes held on a Saturday morning." Samuel replied, "Yes, why not? It will get him out of the house and keep him busy." So mid-week, Anne phoned the teacher and arranged for him to join the class.

Life at school kept Ossie busy, and time flew by with his chorister duties and the art classes. He was always on the go; it seemed they were always buying him clothes and new shoes as his body developed through his teenage years. Nevertheless, Ossie loved Beamont School, and his close bond with his art teacher blossomed.

The teacher did his utmost for Ossie; he was always on hand to give advice. One day Ossie said, "What do you think I should do with my life, Mr Thomas?"

"You stay out of trouble and work hard at school. There will be opportunities if you get your head down and use your time here. Perhaps you can go on to further your education. There will always be a place in the world for designers. I will bring you some magazines to look through."

"Thanks, sir," replied Ossie; he liked the idea. He was still unsure about the direction he would take in his life but knew he must think about his future.

When the school bell clanged, all the kids rushed out of the class to play football. Ossie stayed behind and spoke with Mr Thomas about art and his views on the world. They formed a bond and remained friends for decades. Ossie would listen for hours to Mr Thomas's stories about his life and experiences in the war with his curious mind.

Ossie admired and respected the teacher. However, some other boys resented him and thought he was the teacher's pet. Ossie would laugh and say "Piss off" to the kids who tried to mock him for his friendship with the teacher.

On his thirteenth birthday, June 9th, 1955, his parents bought him a new bicycle. He cycled to school. He was never late and would lock his bike up in the schoolyard and keep his eye out for Mr Thomas when he drove through the school gates. The two got on so well; it was always a pleasure for them to see each other.

Ossie loved sitting at his desk in the art room with a paintbrush between his fingers, showing his illustrations to Mr Thomas, who appreciated the boy's talent. Ossie stayed out of trouble. Boys would brawl outside the school gates, but this wasn't Ossie's style. Instead, his mind was consumed with creativity. The last thing he wanted was to roll on the ground in combat.

Although courageous in his way, he was much more mature than most boys in his class. Ossie could never understand the boys who didn't want to do well. He knew how precious it was to learn and how it could help his future.

He was one of the clever boys who developed ambition and had guidance at an early age. Although he loved a bit of fun and mischief, like most boys of his generation, he was here to absorb and study.

In addition, he was a good-looking boy. Many of the girls in his class thought about Ossie and gravitated toward him at any opportunity. The Bell Hall, a local youth club he frequented, where the legendary DJ Peter Rigby spun the day's records, gave him a love of great bands. Ossie loved music and style. They went hand in hand in his world.

The school taught him architecture, and he learned about geometry. He knew how deep to build foundations. At Beamont, a technical school, boys with practical minds flourished under the proper supervision. They trained him in English and Flemish bonds; he knew the variance. This was something a good bricklayer or architect would know about.

In 2022, Tony Jefferies, a year below Ossie, recalled a conversation about bicycles. Tony was a cyclist, and Ossie admired his bike. Tony was keen on art, and amazed at Ossie's talent. Ossie gave him a pencil drawing of a table with a lamp. Unfortunately, he no longer has the picture. In short, Ossie's talent was appreciated.

Tony left Beamont Technical School in 1959 with one 'O' level, in Art. He remembered that Mr Thomas would hurl pieces of chalk at you if you didn't pay attention. It was a strict school; he remembered the metalwork teacher Jack Atherton punching a student so hard on the chin that he knocked him out. Also, one classroom was separated in the middle, with half the room learning Geography whilst the other half studied History. Tony left with one 'O' level, and the teacher said he would never get a job, but he became a chief executive in the public sector, qualified as a barrister, and earned a master's degree in Public Sector Management. How much of his success he could put down to Beamont is questionable.

I, for my part, left the school in 1974 and can confirm how brutal the teachers were.

Some thought Ossie was a bit shy and aloof. Still, he became a sensation in the art room, and only some could understand him.

With his quick mind and sharpness, it almost seemed natural, the things he did.

Mr Roy Thomas, the Art teacher, with his longish hair, had survived the horrors of a World War Two concentration camp in the Far East. He mentioned he had had hot pins driven into his fingernails by the Japanese.

The kids nicknamed him John Thomas behind his back, slang for penis. Childish, I know, but they were kids. Although when I look back, I still have crazy memories of the school.

With a great love of fashion, charmed by Ossie, the two spent hours together in the storeroom at the back of the classroom. Ossie, with his charisma, drew people into his orbit. He was young and full of vigour.

One day, Mr Thomas entered the class and handed him an extensive *Vogue* and *Harper's Bazaar* fashion weekly collection. "Look through these; remember I talked about these magazines? They can nourish your brain and give you some ideas for your future."

"Yes, thanks so much, sir. I will have a gander."

He sensed Mr Thomas's affection, which made him determined. When a teacher shows interest in your education, and you think it is genuine, a child will respond and do his best to please the teacher.

Some kids go crazy in the school environment and can't focus. Perhaps they rebel and disrupt the class because of the shit they go through at home. This wasn't the case for Ossie. Instead, he flourished under admiration and supervision.

Mr Thomas knew Ossie was exceptional and would thrive under his guidance. Ossie would go home at night and tell his mam about Mr Thomas and their bond; this pleased Anne as she made his tea in the kitchen. It gave her a warm glow. Her boy was in firm hands and she didn't need to worry. The school headmaster, Mr Birkett, said to Ossie that laying bricks was all he would be capable of. How wrong he was.

Ossie pored over the glamorous magazines and flipped through the pages. He fell in love with the fashions of the time. Little did he realise it would become his life's work. Mr Thomas was under Ossie's spell. However, he later said he could teach him nothing about art. "The boy is far too clever and knows much more than I do." Nevertheless, he continued to be Ossie's champion from the early days. He kept on at him with good advice because he knew how special Ossie was.

Mr Thomas spoke with the children in the class. He hid a dark secret, but taking his class was always a pleasure. Although it wasn't something you would think about when you were a kid. It was brilliant to have a teacher pay attention to you and make you feel like he wanted to help you learn. He did it in a fun way, maybe to gain your trust.

However distasteful this may sound, it was a fact in the 40s and 50s: there was no real sex education and as a result children were much more naïve than today's kids. When you're being abused, you don't realise it. Because the children were so gullible with teachers, they wouldn't understand they were being groomed.

Although there is the other side: many pupils would experience their first teenage crush by falling in love with the teacher. After lines became distorted, nobody said much in those days. You kept it to yourself. After all, you thought nobody would believe you or didn't want to get the teacher in trouble, or you got on with it because you knew no different.

These things happened over 50 years ago, but does this mean they shouldn't be mentioned? Jimmy Savile was never exposed because people covered up for him until after his death. Perhaps it continues in schools today, and somebody out there is quiet about it for fear of retribution. It's a crazy world we live in.

In 2022, Diane Bellis, a former classmate of mine, recalled the times when she and some of her friends would go to the home of Mr Thomas, where he plied them with fine wine and snapped photographs of the girls in their school uniforms. Another girl in the class, Anne Trantum, remembers this too. Mr Thomas took an interest in her artwork. He suggested to her mother that she should follow the same route Ossie took. It never happened, although Anne is now still involved with art. He encouraged and got behind the artistic pupils in the class and did his best to make them think about their futures.

Kids went into the back room of the classroom where the art supplies were kept and looked at his magazines. Most thought he was an excellent teacher. He liked boys, never suggesting any improprieties with them, only the girls. They told nobody. Although he had a sadistic side. Still, most schools were like this in the horrific 50s, right through to the 70s when we were there. Mr Thomas would creep about the classroom in his hush puppies and look over your shoulder if you weren't doing as you were told. Then, he leaned over and gave you a hard whack. And it hurt like hell.

Ossie excelled at school and took technical drawing classes with the school bully, a teacher called Knocker Norris, an ogre of a man, or at least he was in my eyes. He became putty in Ossie's hands, though; he couldn't do enough for him. Mr Norris could tell how bright Ossie was.

I think Mr Thomas resented Mr Norris. I wouldn't be surprised if Ossie was his favourite, too. For sure, Mr Thomas introduced Ossie to the world of fashion and his lifelong love affair with style. Lady Henrietta Rous, a close friend of Ossie and confidante, copied and edited *The Ossie Clark Diaries* in 1998 with the permission of his two sons, Albert and George, and their mother, Celia Birtwell. Lady Henrietta wrote about how Ossie became involved in drugs.

Mr Thomas rang Ossie's mother when he left at 15 to persuade him to go to Manchester for further education. Manchester is thirty minutes from Warrington by train; Ossie's mother, Anne, gave him prescription drugs to stay awake for the journey each day. It may seem strange to believe, but I'm sure his mother thought it would help keep him awake and alert and assumed there could be no harm in a bit of stimulation.

Other pupils remember Ossie with mixed emotions. Many people misunderstood him, which is the true mark of a one-off maverick artist. They divide opinions. I wonder if Ossie knew about his sexuality back then. Did he realise he was attracted to both sexes, and did he ignore his male friends?

In the 50s in the north, it could be perilous to admit you were gay. There is an area of Warrington, the toilets in Queen's Gardens - or 'queers gardens' as it became known - where gay men would gather and have sex in the cubicles. Gangs of teenagers would go to the toilets, which had holes bored in the doors, and peer through them. If they spotted a man masturbating or caught in the act with another man, they'd shoulder barge the door, and burst into the toilets, dragging the unfortunate man outside. They would beat him with fists and feet, leaving him half-dead on the floor in a pool of blood.

You would have to be brave to admit you were gay. I can understand why gay guys wouldn't admit to their feelings in this hostile, secretive environment. Things have come a long way since those times - or have they? People still have their prejudices and are quick to point them out, whether behind closed doors or in the streets. These things still go on in small provincial towns across the UK.

Or worse, you could have gone to prison for sleeping with another man and ended up in Strangeways or Walton Jail on protection, in fear for your life throughout your sentence, shunned by the other prisoners and threatened by violence each day.

Ossie was different from most boys his age; in this tough working-class town, he would have to be on his guard about whom he confided in. In later life, he said he loved sex. With his intelligence and curiosity, Ossie wanted to explore the world and all it offered. He didn't want to hang around and do nothing with his life. Somehow, he would make his mark, with aspirations far beyond his hometown.

Under the supervision of Mr Thomas, Ossie finished his time at the school. The five years he spent there helped shape his future. HIs mother wanted him to succeed in life and not become a robot for the local factories; she wanted more for her boy. So she would do all she could to help him get ahead.

"Fashion is not something that exists in dresses only. Fashion is in the sky, in the street; fashion has to do with ideas, the way we live, what is happening."

Coco Chanel

Manchester School of Art

Ossie formed tunnel vision when he left Beamont and sharpened his focus on fashion design, much to the howls of laughter from his school friends.

He'd befriended the mother of his pal Peter Fearon, who told Ossie his mum loved to sew. Ossie met her and absorbed what she taught him. The boy is a natural, she mentioned to Peter. His sister Gladys, whom he studied at home, encouraged him to go for it. Nobody would keep him from his chosen pathway. His mother went to work for the first time and gave up cigarettes to help fund him at art college if he was accepted. The love of a mother is indispensable to any young man's development. She continued to hand-knit jumpers, which he treasured. Anne loved Ossie with a passion, and he returned this love. She would buy wool from the nearby Earlstown market. No wonder Ossie developed a love of ingenuity and an incredible eye for colour. Things don't just happen. Adults inspire a boy's mind; in Ossie's case, his mother and sister inspired him. In the 50s, they would consider you a Nancy boy if you started sewing and dressing dolls. This didn't seem to bother Ossie one bit. He found his direction in life. He was one of the lucky ones, who would escape the drudgery of graft in the local factories scattered throughout the town.

Ossie studied pattern cutting before he became a designer. That's why his clothes were such a good fit. This gave him the edge over other designers, recalled Julie Kueres in 2022.

Ossie worked at various menial jobs for ready cash. He worked for a brief time at Crossfield's in Warrington, the soap factory, a large, corrugated building that seemed to pump out white soap suds 24/7 behind Bank Quay railway station. Ossie went there for a while in quality control. He also worked as a butcher's assistant, scrubbing the blocks with a wire brush after school, and as a petrol pump attendant on the weekends.

He disliked the work and felt this was beneath him. Who could blame him, if you were unlucky enough to spend the next forty years there? Countless, enthusiastic hands did, however. Warrington was renowned for its manufacturing works, which sucked many teenagers into a life of toil and perhaps a gold watch at the end of their servitude. But at least you were guaranteed a job for life, a rare thing in the 21st century.

Ossie's application to study at Manchester Regional Art College, founded in 1838, was accepted, on the recommendation of Mr Thomas. Now part of Manchester Metropolitan University, it's the second oldest art school in the UK after the Royal College of Art in London, which was established in 1837. In 1958, the college in Manchester accepted Ossie, aged 16, on the strength of his illustrations without a portfolio. The teachers recognised his rare ability. At the start of term, he strode aboard the train at Warrington Central station, in one hand his ticket and in the other his coloured pencils, full of hope, with electrified vitality surging through his teenage bloodstream.

As the train chugged from Warrington to Manchester's Oxford Road train station, he settled into his seat. He was edgy and excited at the prospects ahead; this was a considerable move in the right direction for his career.

Most teenagers wanted to be like their peers or went through a rebellious period. Ossie was light years ahead of many. He tried to set trends, not follow them. After an introductory duration, he established himself at the college. The roots of his talent can be traced back to this college, renowned in the north of England alongside Salford and Bradford colleges.

Over the years, he would have to pick up everything about fashion design, envisioning a concept and following it through every step, sourcing the material and assembling it into an interconnected format. In addition, he would have to have a knack for sewing. And he was conveying his ideas to fruition. He had to multitask, and have an extraordinary vision. You must think out of the box to get anywhere in the world of fashion.

Ossie was flexible, curious, studious, and ambitious, all the things needed to succeed in his life. But he would have to gain more experience, and the college would help him with all this at the outset of his mission.

Two of his tutors, Miss Tyrer and Miss Ryder, were interested in his development. They encouraged Ossie to improve his natural ability. So, for example, he would pick up how to strand a needle, and he stayed late a couple of nights a week until 9pm; he was taught by a tailor who came to teach the class at night. This showed his dedication. He learned all he could. As a result, Ossie was well-educated with the practical skills which would be the fundamentals of his later works.

Manchester was prosperous, with the finest shops and latest fashions, far more so than Warrington. He went on an enchanted, mysterious tour around the city. He loved his time at the college.

Indeed, it's a place full of imaginative thinkers, the north. Ossie stood out with his quick wit and self-assurance.

Celia Birtwell was born in Bury on the 22nd of March 1941. Her mother had been a seamstress, and her father was an engineer who loved culture. Celia studied textiles and pottery at Salford School of Art in 1956, and was brought up in Prestwich, and was filled with ambition. She wasn't a chatterbox - she was shy and reserved, but also practical and down to earth.

Celia applied to Salford Art School aged thirteen and passed the exam. Thus, she showed an aptitude for the arts from an early age. This is where she met her best mate, Mo McDermott. The pair hit it off and went on many adventures around Manchester in the late 50s. Mo loved to party and would take speed in the clubs of Manchester, and he made Celia laugh with his devil-may-care attitude.

Mo told Celia about Ossie after he left Salford and went to study with Ossie at the Manchester Regional College of Art. Ossie fascinated him, and he said to Celia," You must meet him." They met for the first time in 1959, and the pair struck up a friendship.

Celia brought Ossie home to meet her mother, who had so much knowledge from her old job as a seamstress, and she helped Ossie make clothes. They partook of many tête-à-têtes. She used to say to Celia: "This boy is gifted."

Celia went to Warrington and met Ossie's mum and dad, and the family members who were still at home. The pair grew closer and became firm friends. Ossie began calling Celia 'Beakie', as young people do when they forge a deep connection and have their language between themselves.

When Ossie thought about their first get-together, he had been struck by Celia's beauty. He could tell she was bright and not in the least stuck up. She carried herself like a lady. Style oozed out of her. Celia passed muster in Ossie's eyes. He wanted to get to know her better.

The first thing that hit Celia about Ossie was how confident and self-assured he seemed. She could tell he had a lust for life, dressed well, and knew he studied at the college. He could well be someone she could get along with. It would take time before they got to know each other. They weren't intimidated. Celia was careful about whom she mixed with, in any case. He would have to prove himself first.

They would meet around the city in various coffee shops or the Twisted Wheel, bounce ideas around, and have fun. One can only imagine the banter they must have had.

I've tried to capture Ossie's personality from the early years as we trace his life from childhood. He could light it up when he entered a room; he appeared to ooze charm, he had manners, and an intuitive mind. Ossie projected all three, recalled his first girlfriend, Jenny Dearden, who knew Ossie when he was 14. He used to make her dresses and became very protective. Women crave a man who will stick by and care for them. He wore round collars and winkle-picker shoes; he was insanely handsome.

Still, Ossie was nobody's fool and wouldn't waste his time on certain people; another sign of a man on a mission. He was forthright and straight to the point. He could infuriate people with his caustic wit if he homed in on them. I'm sure this made him more energetic and entertaining to his friends.

I can see Ossie's character forming. He was young, hip, and tuned in to the ideas of the day. He'd spent years thinking about his dreams. Yes, he must have made people angry along the way, but no matter what, he wanted out of Warrington: his eye was on the main chance and dreams could be made a reality in London. He listened to Radio Luxembourg; he was informed about world events and the day's music. He had a thirst for knowledge.

In 1960, aged 18, he took the first of many excursions to do some work experience overseas at Christian Dior in Paris. Friends and family threw in cash to fund his trip. He was buzzing to get the chance to watch up close in one of the world's top fashion houses. It must have been like a dream come true. He was in awe, working in the full salon's back room. He could watch how the business worked and spot the wealthy clients surrounded by these fabulous dresses. The customers bought them without a thought about how much they cost; it was a world away from his northern background. He came back motivated and enthused by the trip.

In the same year, he took his first trip to London. He hitchhiked from Pops 'transport café in Warrington, a trucker's pit stop serving meals to the lorry drivers, a wonderful place to hitch a ride from. He stood outside the car park with a piece of cardboard with 'London' scrawled in black ink.

A lorry squealed to a halt and the driver wound his window down. "Come on, lad, jump in. I'm on my way towards London."

Ossie climbed aboard and flopped himself down for the 220-mile journey, which seemed to take forever; they arrived eight hours later.

When the driver dropped him off, he went to see his friend Mo, who had recently moved to London. They went around the city together for a few days. Ossie mentioned in his diaries that a Jewish hairdresser tried to rape him in a flat in Maida Vale; he fought him off, and legged it out of there. However, with his striking looks, chicken breast, white skin and long black hair, which framed his handsome face, Ossie drove both men and women wild with lust.

He stayed with his sister Kay and laughed about the escapade when he met up with Mo, who knew the guy. But, of course, it wasn't unusual for young men to go to London and hawk their arse to the highest bidder, something Ossie never did, much to the amusement of his school friends, who had their suspicions. Kids in the north could be vicious if they suspected you were homosexual. The next day he dashed over to see Marlene Dietrich at the Queen's Theatre on Shaftesbury Avenue, in the heart of the West End. The show was magnificent; Ossie loved the atmosphere of glamour as Marlene sang 'Look me over closely'. He said everybody in the audience did. When the curtains opened, she stood in a see-through dress, and people's mouths were agog; it was so unbelievable that the effect would stay with Ossie for the rest of his life. He had a great time in London and looked forward to another trip.

A few days later, he returned to Manchester and continued his studies. He was the only man on the course. He would have loved the attention. Who wouldn't?

In his second year at the college, the local press spotted him. The *Evening Chronicle* printed a story about his progress. His photograph appeared in the paper with his mod haircut, and an innovative collarless suit jacket without buttons and lined with silk. The Beatles would later wear this style, which became more prevalent in 1963. It showed how far ahead of the game he could be.

His achievements at Manchester exposed his genuine flair for drawing and his gift for transforming ideas into three-dimensional forms. Although, admittedly, the preparation he learned was more technical than design. Still, it gave him the skills of a significant cutter and would stand him in good stead.

At this time, in Germany, in August 1961, the East German police and volunteers were constructing the Berlin Wall. A rough-and-ready barbed wire and concrete fence divided one side of the city from the other. The purpose of the wall was to keep the so-called 'western fascists' from entering East Germany. But it stemmed from the tide of mass defections from the east to the west. The rest of Europe saw it as a sign of subjugation, making worldwide headlines. It was all over the media, and many students across the country discussed the event for months. Ossie was full of curiosity and determined to make a success. The girls on Ossie's course wore miniskirts in 1961, long before they became fashionable in London five years later. When Mary Quant brought them to the fore, she named them the mini after the Mini cars of the day.

So far, Ossie had made all the right moves, almost like someone destined him for greatness, the chosen one. He made it happen with his dynamism. Getting there was vital to him. He probably never over-thought what would happen when he achieved his plans. The teachers encouraged him to take the entrance exam for the RCA in London. He had to apply soon because the age limit was 22.

The main thing he had to do was head to London for the interview and impress the tutors. After this, Ossie would have a place to stay with his sister Kay in the capital. He took the entrance exams for the RCA, which involved making toiles, a cheap mock up of a dress made with calico or muslin before creating it with expensive fabrics, and pattern design, and a general knowledge test, to evaluate the student's mind. There was an incisive discussion afterwards. Ossie passed, and they awarded him a scholarship of £330 a year, which helped with his expenses.

Janey Ironside recalled that Ossie seemed somewhat overconfident at the interview. His friend Stevie Buckley remembered he wasn't confident, just sharp, making him look overconfident. This would mask his true feelings when he wasn't feeling self-confident.

When his term was over in Manchester, he graduated. He was more than ready to put the next stage of his plan into action. I can imagine the excitement as his mother packed his clothes and bade him farewell and he took the train to London. I am sure she was sad to see her youngest child leave, but also excited for him at the same time. It leaves a big hole in a woman's life when the kids leave the family home, as they must. It was time now for Ossie to explore his options in the capital. As the London train chugged into Euston Station, four hours later (the trains were slow in those days), he went to find the tube station for his destination. He checked the tube map to see which line he would have to get on. He took the Victoria Line, changed at Oxford Circus, and then took the Bakerloo Line to Maida Vale. He rushed off in the direction of the underground and waited for the train, which squealed to a halt a few minutes later.

When the tube train's doors opened, he stepped inside with the crowd of people laden with suitcases and plonked himself down. He took the 25-minute journey to Maida Vale, bag in hand, full of confidence.

"We must never confuse elegance with snobbery."
Yves Saint Laurent

London

Ossie was thrilled to arrive, full of positivity and eager to join the college. He left the station, carried his suitcase and bounced up the steps to stay with Kay. She lived in an attractive area of West London, close to Little Venice, Paddington, and Bayswater. This was an excellent place to live, and it took the financial worries away until he found his own home.

Kay sang in jazz bands; by now, she'd lived in London for years, so she knew her way around the city. Ossie would design outfits for Kay to wear on stage to enthral the punters with her stage presence. And she would have done what she could to make him welcome and help him settle.

The 60s got off to a quiet start. Ossie arrived at the right moment. He and his friends would be the force behind the 60s fashion. The hemlines on the girls, by the mid-60s, barely concealed their panties.

His friends Mo and Celia also lived in London. Celia secured a summer job in a coffee bar called Hades and remained because she relished London life so much. It was a buzz. David Hockney had finished at the Royal College. He lived upstairs of the pub Hennekeys, on Portobello Road, at the centre of the thriving art scene; Peter Blake, the artist, drank there. David Hockney himself was an innovator.

Hockney wore bright apparel in the 60s and was openly gay. His paintings reflected the clothes he wore. His hair was black, although he wanted to stand out on one of his first visits to New York. He saw an advert on the television for women's hair dye that used the catchphrase "blondes have more fun", so he dyed his hair champagne coloured. In addition, he wore jackets matched up with vivid colours. He was confrontational about his gayness. He wasn't going to hide it; he became fearless, with an 'I don't care' attitude about what people thought of him. This audacious statement about homosexuality was yet to be legalised. Hockney was young and clever, courageous and unafraid, and his clothes, like his art, hit you in the face and assaulted all your senses. I imagine he would have been a crazy sight as he strolled on Portobello Road, with the Jamaicans and the working-class Irish labourers who frequented the area in those days.

It was a liberation for him to come from his background in the north of England, and many would soon copy it in the years ahead. Ossie and Hockney were drawn to each other when Mo introduced them. Hockney loved Ossie for his appreciation of art and clothes. They encouraged each other. A beautiful friendship would stem from these early days together.

Celia lived in a room on Addison Road in the Notting Hill/Ladbroke Grove area of west London. She'd rented the space from the antique dealer John Manasseh. It was great for Ossie to have good friends in London's newly recognised avant-garde art scene.

Life would have been sensational and heady after the drudgery of the north. I'm sure he was driven to explore everything on offer and determined to do well on the course to get ahead in life. So now, he came into a circle of established friends. Their connections made life much easier for a new arrival to the smoke, as London was known when he arrived. I'm sure Ossie took it all in and devoured all he could.

The museums, the art galleries, the markets, the people, and the mixture of colour and cultures must have inspired his creative juices to the extreme. Much like the trips he took to Paris whilst still a student at Manchester a few years earlier, he saw Coco Chanel and Pierre Cardin working in Dior's house for three days. They opened his mind to a world of glamour he yearned for.

The first day at the Royal College of Art, the world's most prestigious art and design college, he must have felt he had arrived already. He couldn't fail to be impressed by his surroundings, opposite Hyde Park. Nestled up close in the shadow of the Albert Hall was the principal place the students studied; although the fashion department was further away in a building opposite the Victoria and Albert Museum, on the third floor of number 3 Cromwell Road in South Kensington, in those days.

The RCA was established in the 40s. When Ossie arrived, a 43-year-old first-ever woman was professor of fashion design. Janey Ironside was in control of the college and Ossie adored her. She was a crucial figure in empowering fashion to be recognised as a practical educational subject in the United Kingdom.

He only saw her twice in his first year. She arrived at 11.30 in the morning, revitalised by a glass of gin to face the students. It exhilarated Ossie to study under her tuition. When Janey wrote her life story, she defined Ossie as one of her most talented students, interested in pop ideas but drawing his inspiration from the past.

People in haute couture taught the fashion design course and mass-market creation. In addition, there were lectures in philosophy, and the history of art and fashion. To close, an excellent all-around instruction educated them on tailoring and working on a toile.

In those days, the classes were small, perhaps fifteen students. So you had to be on top of your imaginative intelligence. There were lavish parties in the college bar every Friday, which could go on all night; Ossie could be a great friend as they danced around to the latest songs of the day.

Everybody wanted to be there, and people who weren't students would turn up because it was a centre of originality. Ossie valued the college. His talents were recognised and encouraged to the maximum. It was a brilliant time to be young and alive through the sexual revolution. The women had the pill, so young people engaged in casual sex, men and women looked genderless, and either sex could fancy you.

These were sensational, powerful days. Indeed, Ossie must have been in his element. London was energetic with its newfound verve, with the young creatives at its centre. The fashion editors of the day looked to the RCA to see the next important thing in style. Ossie was more than ready to work his butt off to get ahead.

He wasn't there to mess around. He loved the academy's atmosphere and wanted to impress his tutors. So, each year, he made friends with all the students. He would wander around the college with his designs inserted under his arm, conversing with fellow students at their desks.

To be open is a northern trait, and it wouldn't have been difficult for him to charm people and engage in discussion. His first year was smooth. He wouldn't do it if he didn't want to do something, though he had an attitude and was a dissident when it took his fancy.

He found the work they assigned him somewhat easy. Some students would struggle for weeks to create what Ossie could do overnight and make it look cool. Yet, pooled with his flair, his flashes of inspiration seemed natural. He just had this in abundance.

He was fluent and made sketches and drawings of his latest creations. London was the city to be in. Ossie arrived at the right moment in time. His mind hungered to absorb as he explored the city. A true Gemini. He needed stimulation, and with all on offer, he would dive in headfirst, full of enthusiasm, with an insatiable drive to learn.

Ossie had dreams and desires. I can envision a single-minded man who needed to prove himself to his tutors and students. He, without hesitation, was a one-off. Mystic, spiritual, authentic, astute, outside his age. He would have to be unique to stand out in such a company of innovative young minds of the 1960s. They were drawn from all around the UK and the world.

He was ahead of the game with his God-given talent. I know he was in his element. There must have been get-togethers, music, girls and drugs galore; he was encircled by extraordinary people at 20 years of age. What more could a boy want? He prepared the tasks assigned to him with great focus and oomph. He was dexterous and knew how to sew—he fixed the whole shebang without a problem. The practical technical background he came from held him in good stead.

There were classes in shoe design, millinery, belt design and tailoring. In addition, the students took life drawing classes, which enhanced their ability to create three-dimensional projects. Everybody grasped that Ossie was the most fantastic pattern cutter, packed with flair, in his year.

He was also clear-cut competitive with colossal self-assurance, and he motivated and elevated the standards of his classmates. He scoured magazines and took in all he spotted or heard on the streets of London. As a result, his mind was stimulated and open to new ground-breaking ideas.

Ossie made friends fast in the tutorial room. He was bold and instinctive. Ossie would work on designs nobody else could think of. When designing, he was always meticulous. He had marvellous energy and could think outside of the box. Ideas flowed from his mind onto the paper. He understood the feminine form and knew how the clothes would look. Perhaps this had something to do with his feminine side.

The college took the students to the magnificent Victoria and Albert Museum. Ossie took great stimulation from past designs. His eyes took it all in. The teacher Bernard Neville, an active textile designer, writer and historian, wanted to open their eyes to the historical past in clothing and the vast potential of future fashion design. They would examine old toiles to observe the cut. This revelation inspired Ossie.

He took great delight in the trips to the museum and believed Mr Neville was an exceptional teacher. He would set them a project to study Dior or Chanel. He asked the students to do sketches from contemporary magazines and photographs. He would show the undergraduates what inspired him, and this became more of a stimulus to Ossie, looking at the dresses of historical periods in the museum. I believe a jigsaw puzzle came together in Ossie's mind and made things much more apparent. He grasped how to make fantastic designs.

Ossie loved to read the bound *Vogue* magazines of the twenties and thirties. He thought, why couldn't we transform this into today's streetwear? He put this all down to Bernard Neville, who made him feel this way. He was happiest when he wandered around the museum, drawing inspiration.

To study this unique epoch, Ossie bought Mae West's diaries, published in the 60s. Mae West was one of Ossie's favourite women. With her unusual look and fearlessness, he found her captivating. This gave him the idea to begin his diaries in later life.

In his second term at the RCA, Ossie shone even more. He would take longer on his creations, and the tutors noticed. Pierre Cardin had enthused Ossie in Paris. He entered a competition for the *Sunday Times* with his women's designs, but he also entered a few men's sketches at the last moment. It was the menswear competition that made him a winner.

He still saw his northern mate Mo McDermott, the quick-witted gay friend who brought the visionary genius of Ossie and Celia together years before. He posed for life modelling for the artist David Hockney, which must have transformed Ossie's thoughts on homosexuality. Ossie had displayed no interest in this way of life in the past, though, and maybe suppressed these thoughts in the north.

Celia lived in Ladbroke Grove, home of the notorious slum landlord, the Polish-born Peter Rachman, who died in November 1962, not long before Ossie arrived in the city of thrills. Ossie would visit her often. He fell in love with the area and the world-famous market on Portobello Road fired up his ingenious vein. He discovered dresses on the market which influenced the bias cut, the method of cutting on the diagonal grain at 45 degrees of the material rather than the straight and cross grains. The procedure causes the fabric to fall and drape to create a catlike shape. Ossie later took this process to another level. It was first developed by the Parisian couture Madeleine Vionette in 1927. The cut causes the dress to caress the curves and delicately flow. To cut on the bias took an incredible amount of skill and patience; if not sewn correctly, the dress can bunch and twist. Ossie would take these garments home and study how the dresses were constructed.

The Portobello Market was one of his favourite places. Stallholders would shout out to the customers, the sounds of music came from the buskers lined up, and down the road, the smell of fried food would assault the senses. You never knew what you could find on the stands. And he loved the vibe of the hub of Notting Hill, which can be compared to a village deep in the heart of the Royal Borough of Kensington and Chelsea.

The market stretched over a mile from Notting Hill Gate, meandering through hundreds of stalls down Golborne Road. Ossie was in his element. He stopped at the pub Hennekeys for a quick drink. Thousands of tourists would wander down the Bella on a busy Saturday. It was crammed with performers and day-trippers from across the globe. They were all hunting for bargains and souvenirs from their London visit.

They watched the stallholders lay out their wares, searching for a unique item to show their friends and neighbours what they bought on their trip to the Bella. The competition was stiff; everybody was looking to make or save a pound.

The atmosphere even now is incredible; day-trippers are dazzled by the inconceivable colours and the chaotic movement of the crowds. They amble through the Bella, craning their necks and speaking diverse vernaculars, all mixed to form a magical cinematic experience, imprinted on first-time visitors 'brains as they bump through the crowds of tourists and locals. The affluent and working-class rub shoulder to shoulder, looking for antiques and preferred vegetables to consume over the weekend.

Ossie would lean over, finger, scrutinise items, and pluck them from the stalls along the packed streets. The smell of meats and hamburgers sizzled through the air as he jostled with the crowds. Later, he would merge old bits and pieces with new ones, to harvest foundations of innovativeness to be used in the lecture room. He fast gained status as a rebel who did things his way.

Ossie fell for Celia's beauty, but I'm sure her level-headedness and northern roots helped too, and they had a lot in common. He visited her room in Ladbroke Grove. Four years after the race riots of 1958, the Caribbean population was over 100,000 and it was an exciting place to live. And this get-together of two great minds was on the way to taking a romantic turn.

Ladbroke Grove was a multicultural area filled with people from all over the world, where you could be yourself. They outgrew their northern sensibilities and went on an exciting journey together. The area had much to offer, close to Central London, Chelsea, and South Kensington. I'm sure these were exciting days for these two young people, both on a mission to succeed in their chosen careers.

The college was excellent for Ossie to use his thoughts and bounce concepts around with vivid imagination. Janey Ironside, who became good friends with all her students, encouraged and brought out the best in them all.

Ossie loved music, and this was the 60s, when drugs altered and opened the minds of the nation's youth. Many social restraints burst wide open at this time of massive change. All it offered must have made it exciting to be young and alive. It would have been impossible to say no to drugs with his background. He lapped them up. A life of glamour and get-togethers of different worlds would surely go to anybody's head.

The ego boost it gave must have been heady. With a head full of ideas, originality overflowed in his brain. Celia found it hard to keep him grounded; I'm sure she tried, but boys will be boys. In the nadir of the coldest winter in 200 years, Ossie went back to Warrington to spend Christmas with the family.

He must have enjoyed the time away from the college and the excellent food his mother made that Christmas of 1963. He stayed for two weeks and returned in January 1964, well-fed and ready to continue his studies. The Thames was frozen solid. The kids wore ice skates and had a blast slipping and sliding across the mighty river.

Ossie was glad to be back in London. He wanted to continue his studies and couldn't wait to return to the classroom. He missed his friends and the tutors 'encouragement. The weekends were great; they had their bar with subsided drinks. Bands and DJs played there.

He first encountered Charlie Watts, the drummer of The Stones, in the student bar, where the scholars gathered to have fun and discuss their respective courses. All kinds of people on the hunt for action would frequent the bar over the weekends. It was rammed out with good-looking undergraduates looking for a bit of fun, and if you got lucky, you might end up in bed with one of them.

Charlie and Ossie got along as they chatted about music and fashion. Charlie was into his clothes big time, and Ossie loved the music of The Stones; they had much to discuss. Ossie went to bed with a hangover that night.

As the winter months passed, Ossie and Celia took a trip to Paris in the summer, mistaken for clients at Chanel. They increased their horizons and soaked up the atmosphere of the fashion houses. This must have spurred them on.

Ossie loved the RCA and forged contacts and friendships with all the leading lights of the day, which proved invaluable in the years ahead.

Ossie was older in the head than most and more mature, and I put this down to his family. He must have learned so much from them. He could hold his own with anybody in a conversation, and was full of confidence and vitality. His aura and cheek mesmerised his friends. London was stirring from its post-war austerity, and all things were possible if you were young and had your finger on the pulse. The Stones and The Beatles are blasting out through the radio.

Or you could, by chance, bump into them in one of the London nightclubs they frequented. The young and rich who flounced about the borough of Kensington and Chelsea fluttered from their houses to their country mansions, thinking they were ahead of life. They were confronted by these working-class oiks, who were much hipper and more fun. Ossie looked like one of The Beatles, playful, attractive and charismatic with his bluish-grey eyes and slight frame. Ossie intrigued people with his northern accent, which could be helpful as the women loved it; he dressed like an artist and turned heads as he strolled through the corridors.

Luckily, good fortune cascaded down on him and his friends. They were in the right place at the right time. London was at the top of the cities across Europe. It drew young bands and writers from around the UK. Anything was possible. Record deals, cash, women, parties, adventure and sex and more sex; surpluses of creative minds flocked to the capital, ready to party and have fun.

Teenagers grew their hair, the old short back and sides outdated. You can imagine the excitement crackling through the air. London must have felt like you were at the epicentre.

The West End, with Soho, where the whores and wide boys plied their trade, dazzled and lured youngsters by the thousands. The notorious meat rack was in Piccadilly Circus, where rent boys hung out searching for an old queen to fill their mouths and empty their wallets for a quick blow job or take one up the arse around the corner behind some deserted restaurant down the back alley.

The junkies and lowlife cruised the area to score or pick up their script from the 24-hour Boots chemist. Idlers lay outside the statue of Eros on the steps. Everybody was out for a thrill. The weekends were the favourite hunting ground of the night's characters amongst the pickpockets and small-time criminals who congregated en masse to make the area buzz.

Ossie took all this in and loved the city's freedom, where he could be himself. A new world opened in front of his eyes. He heard the stories of World War Two, when soldiers from across the globe came to the party with the whores who lined the capital's streets. The squaddies never knew if they would survive the next battle or bombing campaign. They weren't going to miss a quick bunk-up.

Soho was spectacular; many people loved the war for all the hedonism it brought to the bomb-damaged streets of the capital. Easy pickings with blackouts and con artists on every corner to blag and rip people off—a mug on every road, waiting to be relieved of their cash.

As he wandered around discovering the city, Ossie became more absorbed in what went on in the capital's streets. His eyes roamed all over the day's youngsters going about their business. He noted how they dressed, what shoes they wore, and how short their skirts were.

As a fashion design student, it was imperative to be observant and nourish his mind with creativity. Everything was an inspiration. He wasn't one of those who walked around with his eyes closed. It gave him a never-ending supply of ideas back in the classroom, with much to take in.

The city inspired and enthralled him. It was a constant source of stimulation. He took long walks with Celia, and they both pointed things out and motivated each other. They loved the city and went all over London in their quest for fun and adventure.

Jimi Hendrix came to town and partied with Keith Moon, Mick Jagger, John Lennon, Keith Richards, and Paul McCartney, surrounded by hangers-on and drug dealers, glamorous women ready to groove; who couldn't dig this? The 60s may not have been so swinging for the sweatshop workers up north; Ossie escaped by sheer talent and determination.

All this was repeated thirty years later, when Oasis burst onto the scene and Liam and Noel took over London, surrounded by dazzling women like Kate Moss and Sadie Frost, and partying around Primrose Hill and Belsize Park. They made it cool to be a northerner.

People had been coming to London for centuries to seek fame and fortune. After all, weren't the streets supposed to be paved with gold? But it is a life of hard work and struggle in the rat race for many Londoners. Then, at last, music and fashion exploded all over the city, and the chosen few took full advantage.

Ossie couldn't fail to be inspired by the bands of the time. He bought albums by the shedload in the summer of 1964. Ossie won a shoe design competition. The prize money was £150, and Ossie went to Northern Ireland for a few weeks to work at the shoe factory in Banbury.

When he returned, David Hockney was about to embark on a trip to America. But first, to teach for a summer term in Iowa, Ossie spent the £150 he won for the shoe design. David asked him to come, and they took an exciting trip to Chicago and drove through Route 66 to Los Angeles.

Hockney, five years older than Ossie, must have taken charge, and Ossie went along. The collision of two great minds from similar backgrounds exploded into a brief homosexual relationship if the day's rumours were anything to go by.

They wandered around LA. This opened Ossie's eyes wider; stimulation dripped from the streets if you took notice, and for sure, the eyes of a designer would notice it all. Ossie met the actor Dennis Hopper, whom I've admired for years, from the film *Blue Velvet*. He had a starring role as Frank Booth, the psychopathic drug dealer. Ossie also met the most exceptional actress of the day, Bette Davis.

Ossie was mobbed at the Hollywood Bowl when mistaken for George Harrison from The Beatles, which must have been fun.

Then they went onwards to NYC, where he met Andy Warhol and his entourage at the Pop Factory. The Velvet Underground Warhol opened an art studio and painted it silver, known as the Factory. It became a place to hang out for the musicians and the wealthy of the day. Lou Reed wrote a song about it, 'Walk on the Wild Side', about the transvestites and hustlers he met who hung around the place snorting drugs and fucking each other randomly.

It was the place to be seen, where you could make the right connections. And this is where Ossie first met Diana Vreeland, *Vogue*'s editor-in-chief; he was thrilled to meet her. *Vogue* was the world's leading magazine on fashion and style. It began in the late 19th century. Diana had a massive influence in the fashion world, especially in America, where the magazine was founded. There was a *Vogue* Britain office and one in Paris, the birthplace of couture.

Vogue was regarded as the style bible, read by many women worldwide. Diana had an exceptional eye for talent and recognised Ossie as a rising star; they shared a love of ballet and haute couture. They talked about fashion for hours, and she was impressed by Ossie's knowledge, and the two exchanged numbers.

Ossie seemed infused with stardust and to be in the right place at the right time with his journey into fashion and couture. Diana Vreeland was a gift from God in Ossie's life. She was the High Druidess of Fashion and not somebody you could expect to meet every day. By now in her 60s, she was a force to be reckoned with. She had an eye for observation and liked what she saw in this young Englishman, and would support Ossie's work in America over the years to come. He didn't want everybody to dress the same; he hated this. He wanted to create beautiful gowns with a passion, one off pieces, and transform the women of the day into goddesses.

The cost of a couture dress was high, but he believed it was worth the price. Moreover, Ossie was in his element in America. He loved the thrill of the American cities. He discovered so much about the country, and couldn't wait to return to London and convert his ideas into beautiful eye-catching garments.

While he was in New York, his sister Kay met the Motown crew in London, including Diana Ross and 13-year-old Stevie Wonder. Stevie sat on her knee at the legendary Cumberland Hotel near Marble Arch, famed for the wild night Jimi Hendrix spent in the 60s with women he pulled on the streets of London. In 2010, the hotel constructed a room on the fifth floor and called it the Jimi Hendrix Suite in memory of his death 40 years before. It's the Cumberland, Great Cumberland Street, London W1H7DL, if you fancy a night there. The Hard Rock brand took the hotel over in 2019, but it is still worth visiting.

Still, Ossie couldn't stop thinking about Celia. He rang her from New York to tell her how much he missed her and looked forward to seeing her when he got back. He wished she was there to share the experience. They were great friends; Celia must have been wise and far more grounded than Ossie. When the plane landed at Heathrow, he rushed to see Celia on his return. He couldn't wait to tell her all about the trip. Ossie was buzzing with ideas and jumped at the chance to implement them.

Ossie asked Celia if he could move in to split the rent, perhaps out of convenience, as many people who live in London still do. Notting Hill was a fantastic place for creatives and bohemians to live in those days.

The area had a reputation for prostitution. The girls would pick up their clients in the pubs or sleazy basements and take them back to their rooms for a couple of hours to service them and fleece their wallets. Close to the West End, there was never a shortage of potential customers looking for a quick fix of sex and drugs, which were available on the streets of Notting Hill at a price. No cash, no gash. Criminals were always out on the hunt for money, breaking into houses along Holland Park Road or shoplifting in Knightsbridge to fund the life of debauchery they wanted.

Still, this added to the atmosphere of the region. It gave it a sense of danger and perhaps a thrill to mingle with the confidence tricksters and dodgy characters that made this part of London their home. It was a revelation for both Ossie and Celia and they would never forget their early days around the manor.

They spent many happy days wandering around the magnificent Victoria and Albert Museum, drawing inspiration; Celia loved the medieval area, with her art school background. She noticed everything and was a big fan of Coco Chanel, whom they met on one of their trips to Paris in the 60s, when they went to one of her shows. Chanel broke down many barriers and created fashion freedoms that many women take for granted today.

In Ossie's last show at the RCA, the students presented six garments for the degree collection. They held the show in June 1965 at the Gulbenkian Hall inside the Royal College of Art. It turned out to be a spectacular success. A brilliant white dress with fairy lights blinking down the hem was a showstopper and stunned people's minds and made the day's newspapers and black and white TVs. Leon Bakst, a Russian painter and costume designer who designed for the Ballet Russes and died in 1924, inspired them. It was a meteoric rise for Ossie, and the high society of London's fashion world talked about him the next day. Ossie was the only one in his class who graduated in 1965 with a first-class degree. Not bad for a 24-year-old, after four years in London, claiming the respect he so wanted. By the mid-sixties, over 40% of the population was under 25 years of age, and they wanted the latest fashions. Hence, he was perfectly placed to pander to their whims.

London tore into the sixties. Times became fast and more sensational. It must have been difficult for Ossie to handle a few years earlier. Nobody knew who he was. Now his name was on everybody's lips. Would he be able to cope with the fame which came his way? It would help if you worked hard in life, and Ossie made connections that came thick and fast.

Woollands 21 in Knightsbridge, which opened in 1961, was a leading shop that displayed young British designers. Their chief buyer, Vanessa Denza, recalled that half of the problem was that they couldn't find manufacturers who could give them what they wanted. So they went straight to the designers and bought from them. They would put their clothes on the rails in the shop, and they sold out at once. The turnover was incredible, she said. They turned their stock over every three weeks and brought in new clothing all the time. A vibrant figure in the fashion scene, she was brought to lecture the students. She got behind Ossie's creations, which brought him to the buying public at the commencement of his career. Vanessa remembers Ossie sitting at the back of the classroom with a pair of square-faced glasses.

Also, Alice Pollock, who intuitively recognised Ossie's extraordinary talent at the RCA, opened a shop called Quorum in Kensington in 1964 and offered Ossie a job as a designer. Alice and Ossie shared the same birthday, the same day and year. Ossie was ready to dress the pretty young women who moseyed down the King's Road and beyond. Bubbly with ideas and creativity, he couldn't wait to set to work and let the world know about his flair.

He worked from home, and his fantastic talent came up with the most fashionable items in chiffon, snakeskin, and leather. Over time, things took off in a big way. Money poured in.

Quorum's custom shows were known for their magnificence and were popular with the day's celebrities. Ossie's name was on the who's who of the city's elite, and the word would soon spread about his talent and sense of humour. People wanted to meet him and learn more about this young upstart from the north.

The creative talent of Celia and Ossie, combined with their chiffon dresses, enthralled the clients and word spread fast about the gifted pair. Celia created some of the most exquisite fabrics of the era. Ossie used crepe and gauze in a way never seen before. His cut and Celia's prints were inseparable. They were sensual, celestial, and beautiful. Clients wanted them in their scores. Ossie never left home. He wandered in and out when he pleased.

When he hung out with Alice, though, Celia recalled that his character changed. They took drugs together. Drugs were never Celia's thing. Although Ossie loved to indulge, I've been addicted myself, and I know how easy it is to become entangled.

Celia treasured Ossie in the first throes of love. Then, with his quirky sense of humour, he would bring home things for the flat they shared in Ladbroke Grove, vases from the market, and they both settled into their routine.

"In difficult times, fashion is always outrageous."
Elsa Schiaparelli

Notting Hill

In 1965, they shifted to a house on Blenheim Crescent in Notting Hill, close to their flat on St Quinten Avenue. It must have been a relief to have more space to work in. This brought out Ossie's creativity. He went along to the Victoria and Albert Museum, trawling for ideas. The first-ever show he put on while still at the RCA for Alice put them on the map. Now they would have to build on their success.

The pressure built, with fame and money, to stay hip and original. But drugs might have helped Ossie cope, or perhaps he loved the self-indulgent style surrounding him.

1965 was an excellent year for the couple and brought them into contact with the rich and famous of the day. I can only imagine the heights they soared. It must have been adrenaline-charged as an artist to get recognised for your work. And they worked well together, and Celia helped Ossie rise. Of course, textile and fashion designers wouldn't usually get on, but this wasn't the case for this pair. Although they went through their trials and had a difficult time, and split up: Celia went away with Mo McDermott to Greece for six weeks to think things through. When she returned, Ossie kept ringing, and Celia told him it wasn't working out, but Ossie was persuasive. So Celia relented, and they got back together.

England was known for its tweed jackets and cashmere coats in the 1950s. We may have won the war, but we were broke and beaten. The kids of the 50s looked like miniature versions of their parents. However, things changed in the 60s with the fresh, hip young designers, including these two northern go-getters, Ossie and Celia. They were ambitious, with an innate drive to get ahead, and spurred each other on at every stage of the journey.

In Ossie's final year at the RCA, on Sunday morning, January 24th, 1965, he awoke to the news of the death of the former wartime prime minister, Sir Winston Churchill, who'd lain in hospital for 12 days and fought through a series of strokes before this ultimate one ended his life. It was all the students talked about for weeks. Still, life went on. Ossie was super busy with his definitive collection and knew he must make a bold statement; he wanted to electrify and mesmerise his onlookers. He designed a vivid coat with pop art images (he learned a lot on the trip to New York the year before) merged with hallucinogenic material.

David Bailey, the Leytonstone-born photographer, snapped the photos, which appeared on the front cover of *Vogue*. Ossie said he wanted to dress frilly people in colours that confuse the eye.

Wholly modern-day, stark and bold in its apparent simplicity, the creation of the silk satin coat is misleadingly elaborate. Ossie knew what he wanted and was incredible for a man of his tender years, for somebody who'd just graduated. Although Ossie constructed the garment with professionalism, the machine work crisscrossed repeatedly. He was in his element, with the clatter of the sewing machine designing his latest creations. He knew he must give it his all.

In *Vogue*, the photo flashed his image on the front page. Ossie stood beside the British model, the younger sister of Jean Shrimpton and muse of David Bailey, Chrissie Shrimpton. At the time she was going out with the lead singer of The Rolling Stones, Mick Jagger. Chrissie was chosen for her good looks, but the clothes looked good. High-fashion clothes always looked better on skinny models, and Chrissie fitted the bill. Ossie was thrilled to have her in the shoot, and they both looked young and fresh, stuffed with confidence in the photos as they stared into the lens. Ossie knew his journey into the world of style and glamour was about to explode, and he couldn't have been happier.

He was pale and thin with a Beatles haircut. Ossie had arrived. Young, good-looking, and packed with originality, a small but devoted team of creatives working alongside him at Quorum helped build the brand for the public to fall in love with. 1966 was now on the horizon. How exhilarating it must have been: he and Celia were on the road to fulfilling their dreams with money and surrounded by like-minded individuals. They had much to thank Alice Pollock for, and Alice for them.

The man who would later go on to international fame as the guitarist of Pink Floyd, Dave Gilmour, secured a job at Quorum, joining the team as a van delivery driver and he began helping Ossie choose the music for his shows.

Ossie would work late through the night on his creations, with a habit of naming his dresses and never calling them frocks. He hated the word. He christened them terms like Star lapis Ziggy. His originality was endless.

In 1966, Alice founded the male model agency English Boy with Sir Mark Palmer. The latter wanted to change the image of British adulthood, and put the boy instead of the girl on the front cover in the future.

Also in 1966, Ossie and Celia held their first show for buyers on a barge in Little Venice. Their work captivated the editor of *Nova* magazine, Molly Parkin, and Prudence Glynn, the editor of *The Times*. This helped the team become well-known in the media. Friends in high places would never go amiss.

The Windrush generation, who landed in 1948, over 30,000 people from the Caribbean, settled in Britain in Brixton and Notting Hill by the 1950s, the most prominent West Indian population. Trouble flared into riots. In response, the Notting Hill Carnival was born in August 1966. Around 500 people came to the first one, to celebrate Caribbean heritage and stress the diversity in the area. The region is a great place and draws people from everywhere.

Ossie couldn't have failed to notice, although this may have been a culture shock for him from his white working-class background. Still, this only added to London life's excitement and helped spark his creative imagination.

London celebrated in the summer of 1966 when England won the World Cup. They beat their bitter rivals, Germany. It was like we had won the war all over again. This year of great optimism brought the eyes of the world once again to the capital. The beautiful mini-skirted girls of the day captured the imagination of the lusty young men of the nation.

Ossie scoured the city in search of a unique piece of material. His eagle eyes spotted a warehouse in east London where he discovered snakeskin coiled up for 20 years. He reached out to touch it when it leapt back into life. He asked how much it was; 30 bob a foot, or £1.50 in today's money. Ossie saw the potential, hid his eagerness and snapped it up. It was so vast that he made it into a suit, and Linda Keith modelled it.

Ossie knew they had hit the big time when Marianne Faithfull ordered a suede suit trimmed with the python skin and never blanched at the price. She loved to lie around on her Moroccan cushions listening to The Beatles, stoned and dressing up.

Sharon Tate ordered a full-length snakeskin coat with mink lining. Warren Beatty, the stud, was spotted in tight satin trousers, making him look like he was hung like a horse. Women cast admiring glances at Ossie's latest creation.

Clients who wore their python jackets included Keith Richards of The Rolling Stones, Britt Ekland, and Anita Pallenberg. This would have helped sales. The jackets became sought after, and to this day, in 2022, they are classics and can change hands for thousands of pounds.

The day's teenagers looked towards bands like The Rolling Stones and The Beatles and copied their looks. The designers knew this, so it was always good for businesses to get them in your shops and be photographed out on the streets in their latest designs. And the bands looked good with their slight frames, and the clothes brought out the best in them. If you could look like a rock star and attract a good-looking member of the opposite sex, the kids were prepared to pay for it. Fashion is always driven by the youth of the day. It is essential to be seen out on the street looking the part. Some kids would spend their last pound on a beautiful leather jacket or a sheepskin jacket if they saw it on their favourite musician or model.

Quorum moved to Radnor Walk, behind the Chelsea Potter pub off the fashionable Kings Road, a beautiful place to display Ossie's talent for the rich and powerful who frequented the area. It all began with Mary Quant. She used a bold black daisy as her logo, opening her shop in 1955, followed by Dandie fashions, which drew designers to Chelsea and the revolutionary chic Kings Road. It was a place to come and see who wore the latest fashions. You could spot the most outrageous styles on the day's youth like they were on a catwalk. It can't be underestimated how sensational it was if you were young and attractive; it must have felt like being on another planet.

They transported the Flower Power era of San Francisco to London. The kaleidoscope of characters included shaggy-haired beauties with their eyes made up with kohl sauntering along the road towards the World's End. Shops sprang up to cater to the influx of kids. Granny Takes a Trip, another favourite, sold Afghan coats imported from Afghanistan from kids who travelled through Asia cheaply during the 60s on 488 Kings Road. Opened by the designer and artist Nigel Waymouth and his girlfriend, Sheila Cohen, they recruited the tailor, John Pearce. Its unusual designs caught the eye of the rock world, who came to go on a spending spree and didn't recoil at the prices. Inside, they lined the premises with lacy curtains and marble finishes; it was stacked high with silk and satin jackets hung from the rails. At the back of the shop was a jukebox that fed the latest tunes to the kids. It became an experience to hang out there. The stars of the day came there; Salvador Dali, Andy Warhol, and Salman Rushdie used to rent a room above the shop.

Bell bottoms were in fashion; the kids smoked hash and smelled of patchouli oil to mask the marijuana scent they smoked in abundance. Keith Richards and Mick Jagger bought houses on the impressive Cheyne Walk, overlooking the Thames. The Kings Road was indeed fit for a king; a private road was built in 1694, so Charles II could travel from his palace in St James to Hampton Court with ease until the 1800s. Only royalty or aristocrats could use it. King Henry VIII loved the area and he spent decades there. It is still one of the most stylish areas of London to this day and draws people in their multitudes.

Along with Chelsea Football Club, only a brief ride up to Stamford Bridge, you could spot people on the prowl looking for some action. Rock and roll, groovy women, fast motors, sex and drugs - the King's Road was the place to be to grab a slice of the action.

The Chelsea Arts Club, founded in 1890, used to be situated on the Kings Road for its first ten years and was purchased by a group of artists who lived and worked in the area. It later moved around the corner to Old Church Street. Members bought a house there and still catered to the artistic community. It's never short of clientele with subsidised drinks, meals, art shows, and live music events. It is a great place to visit if you can somehow get through the entrance or know a member who can sign you in through its hallowed doors.

Over the other side of the city, Michael Fish, the designer, threw the doors open to his new shop, Mister Fish. His bespoke boutique on 17 Clifford Street, between Saville Row and Bond Street, was open in time for the Christmas sales and frequented by celebrities and the aristocracy, including members of the royal family. He was a contemporary of Ossie, renowned for the kipper tie and dressing the likes of David Bowie in the man's dress for the front cover of *The Man Who Sold The World*. Mick Jagger wore his creation for the 1969 Hyde Park gig as part of the peacock revolution.

Brian Jones from The Stones moved upstairs into a room above Quorum with his girlfriend, Suki Potier. Ossie smoked joints with him, discussing the day's fashion, art, and music. It wasn't long before Ossie gave Brian free clothes, which gave him good karma. Brian told the rest of the band about Ossie and his designs. The Stones bought the clobber, and the word spread. The 60s began swinging, centred around two influential bands, The Stones and The Beatles.

Before long, Ossie and Celia dressed all the elegant people with their fabrics and designs.

Ossie was a striking young man with Celia on his arm when they landed in Paris. The Parisian men stood in the street and gawped at her in sexy sailor pants as she sauntered by; she had a powerful effect on men. Ossie and Celia became a first-class couple of the King's Road in the eyes of the fashionable elite. 400 or 500 handsome guys and gorgeous gals were the mainstays who kickstarted the capital of cool, and who were better placed to dress them than Ossie and Celia? This overused term, 'swinging London', was first coined in *Time* magazine in 1966. There were film crews all over the exotic King's Road, sometimes on both sides. The creative talent of the urban village of Chelsea overflowed with beauty and glamour. It oozed out of the streets. The actor Michael Caine brought his mother to check out the women in their mini skirts.

The thrill of sauntering down the King's Road to shop at Quorum was so trendy that if you went in you could end up locked in there, swallowing champagne and clothed by Ossie, who made you feel like a queen.

Or you could go to Hung on You, situated at 430 Kings Road, opened by Michael Rainey and his wife Jane Ormesby-Gore; all the beautiful people - a term coined by the American editor-in-chief Diana Vreeland - shopped there. Later they would go clubbing in Dell Aretusa, 107 Kings Road, a regular haunt for Ossie, opened by an Italian, Alvaro Maccioni, a members-only club with a disco flashing in the night frequented by the elite: Sammy Davis Junior, The Beatles, The Stones, David Bailey. A two-page spread appeared in the *London Evening Standard*: Are you one of the most Beautiful People? Can you get into this club? It attracted royalty. Princess Margaret and David Bowie became regulars. John Lennon and Yoko Ono had their first public outing there for the pre-launch party for Apple, a new clothes shop on Kings Road. You had to be seen in the scene if you were anybody in the 60s. Everybody wore Ossie Clark, including Celia and Ossie themselves.

Another one of the hip joints in the 60s was the Classic Chelsea Drug Store found at 49 Kings Road, the steel building on the corner of Royal Avenue. It was a massive structure, with clothes and record shops and bars full of the cream of the day's youth strutting around in their peacock-coloured garments, reeking of hash and tripping on acid. The Kinks summed up the 60s with their 1966 hit 'Dedicated Follower of Fashion', which fitted in with the kids who tried to out-dress each other and be the dandy of the decade.

Ossie also drank in the Chelsea Potter and frequented the Pheasantry at 152 Kings Road, a fanciful building that welcomed the young bohemians. It was a ballet academy before it became a restaurant. It was reputed Lauren Bacall and Humphrey Bogart drank in there when they stayed in London. The artist Francis Bacon got pissed in there. Bands performed live gigs.

The Market on High Street, Kensington, a mile or so away, opened in 1967 as a three-storey building. A maze of stalls catered for the nonconformists and the trendies on a tighter budget. Some went shoplifting there, desperate to get their hands on the clobber. Perhaps it was still an incredible buzz - all part of the excitement of shopping in the 60s. Freddie Mercury worked for his bandmate Roger

Taylor, who'd opened a stall in '69 before they became mega-famous as Queen.

Almost 60 years later, London is still a great city in which to live, work and learn about life. People still flock here from across the world. Yes, it may not be the 60s; times move on, and memories linger. But anyone who breathed here will never forget the involvement, good, bad or indifferent. You can't ignore or forget the experience. Some may beg to differ because if you remember the 60s, you weren't there. We can trace the origins of this back to the American Band Jefferson Airplane, who lived through the permissive, hedonistic decade.

In a conversation with Diana Delouche, she relayed a story about Ossie's generosity.

"It was 1964. I was in Alice Pollock's shop, Quorum, where my friend worked. A small, thin young man with lots of hair and a fringe looked in a state. A buyer or someone similar came to view his first collection hung on Alice's rails, and horror of horrors, the red-headed girl supposed to show his dresses let him down. A blonde and a brunette would be there. In those days (thanks to Vidal Sassoon), my hair was auburn, so Alice suggested it to me. It would only be for the morning or afternoon (I can't remember which) and between jobs. They made me walk up and down the shop (tiny and in that courtyard off Smith St). By chance, I had 'done 'a course at Lucy Clayton and could drag a coat behind me without losing it.

"I agreed, and for my payment, I could choose a dress. The buyer came and loved the collection. Ossie was over the moon. Ossie was endearing, easy to get on with, and keen to succeed. So ambitious. I called in from time to time and liked him very much. Then I got caught up in work with no time for wandering down Kings Road, but when I got married in 1966, I remembered his promise to make my wedding dress if I ever got married, in his workshop in Radnor Walk. I need not tell you how fascinating a designer's workshop is with materials, threads, patterns, scissors, and excitable people.

"Ossie became someone of consequence but found time to make a white crepe silk wedding dress cut on the bias with ribbons threaded onto the three-quarter sleeves and around the boat neck. It was straightforward, and he didn't charge me for it. It was the first time I met Celia, and I realised she oversaw the workshop. She said they would sew no label inside the dress because it was free. I had a feeling that, unlike Quorum, someone was IN CHARGE. Alice was a powerful force and helped Ossie deal with everyday life i.e. money, rent, etc. The days of giving away dresses were over. I went to live in Paris with my French husband on my wedding day and heard later with sorrow about Ossie's death. Re: David Hockney's painting of Mr and Mrs Ossie Clark and Percy - it was first shown at the Whitechapel Gallery, run by a friend of mine, Mark Glazebrook, now dead."

I suppose when you don't know much about the fashion trade, you perhaps visualise it as a world of creativity, fizzing with enthusiasm. The designers take great pride in their work, which Ossie did. He worked in the much gentler times of the 60s, before it became a tremendous money-making machine like today, and the competition so stiff, you had to be on top of your game. The seasons come and go. You must churn out clothes for the global markets under severe pressure to be original and unique. Many turn to drinking and drugs to ease the tensions.

Ossie was a one-off, a true nonconformist. He was full of ideas and followed nobody. He landed at the right time. This gave him an outright canvas to create and liberate women like never before. Ossie wanted to create art; it made him feel good inside when he saw the models on the catwalk - he lived for these moments when he could celebrate with his friends in the cut and thrust of the fashion business. He wanted the respect of his peers. I'm sure money was the last thing on his mind. Having the skill to visualise ideas and convey them to fruition made Ossie happy.

He trawled the shops, looking for stimulus. He would select pieces and take them home, then unpick the garments, and check out how they were made. He would draw his inspirations, translate them into his work, and create something special to be paraded on the capital's catwalks.

After the black and white scenes of the 50s and early 60s, in 1967 colour televisions exploded on our screens and captured the majestic streets of the city in all their glory. Abortions were made legal in the UK apart from Northern Ireland. The free love and the pill era let the kids take advantage. The posh hippy-ocrats had the cash and the will to have fun.

Ossie's dear friends Keith Richards and Mick Jagger were busted at Keith's home in Redlands in West Wittering in February '67. They were sent to prison but released on bail a couple of days later. This only added to their bad-boy reputation and did not harm their characters.

The summer of 1967 was the catalyst for things to come. Drugs and mysticism wafted through the air. Everybody stood on an incredible high; maybe not the bankers and politicians, but the lords' and ladies' children. If they weren't, they missed out. To be young and alive in this decade was an experience.

The boutique owners rubbed their hands together when they saw the cash roll in. They came out with sensational clothes, and Quorum, along with Hung On You and Granny Takes a Trip, remained at the forefront.

Mick Jagger and Brian Jones wore Celia's prints on satins and silks. Ossie created men's shirts delicate and frilly in chiffon; in crepe, Mick stood spellbound and draped them around his agile body for his stage shows. This only added to the celebrity of Ossie and Celia, as they "oohed and aahed" around the wealthy young creatures of the day.

One of Celia and Ossie's first designs was for the artistic and flamboyant editor of *Nova* magazine, Molly Parkin. I spoke to Molly at the Chelsea Theatre on King's Road in Chelsea. Now 90 years old, she is still a commanding presence in any room.

I downloaded Molly's autobiography, *Welcome to Mollywood*, which gave me a great few hours of reading. I met her daughter Sophie a few months later at the private members 'club in Aldgate, Vout-O-Reenees, in a crypt below a church. Sophie is a world authority on the Colony Club. She wrote a book on the place. I mentioned that I had read her mother's book, and she said it was fascinating but not her best work. Molly wrote ten books and became the *Sunday Times*'s editor for fashion.

Molly commissioned the Ossie and Celia to make garments for *Nova*. They made paper dresses from home in three assorted sizes.

You could buy them by mail order. Jane Asher, the girlfriend of Paul McCartney, modelled one.

Molly noted how well Celia and Ossie worked together. She thought Ossie might be gay, but they came from the sticks like The Beatles, now all the rage. They were a gorgeous couple, stylish and original.

I'm sure this gave the pair a great buzz. It showed both were headed in the right direction and consumed with the vision to create. They were young and determined. But, still fresh, nothing would prepare Ossie for fame and money. Celia took it all in her stride. They took trips across Europe, and were enthused by the colours and garments of Morocco, Spain and France.

Ossie was now in his fifth year in the capital of dreams. Known as the Trailblazer of the King's Road at 24 years old, he was an animated player in the fashion world with his nimble digits and innovative flair.

Chelsea was chock full of shops and eateries, crammed with life. You could spot John Lennon, Keith Richards, and Ringo Starr wandering the streets, flanked by gorgeous women, their pockets swelled with cash.

London was the centre, much as New York had been. King's Road and Carnaby Street were at the heart of it all. Everyone wanted to be a star. The city was like an electromagnet. Anyone with any nous of style, music or aptitude wished to be here and found themselves drawn to the thrill of this incredible city. National service came to an end in 1960, with post-war economic freedom, and as a result, the kids had more disposable income than their parents.

Mysticism burst and popped with arty stimuli; in abundance, femininity and pills were on hand. The communication was out in the universe. London was the place to be. Glamorous women, the best music, Americans, Africans, Jamaicans, Japanese, and Europeans came by planes, ships, or drove here. They were eager to sample the delights of London town.

Speed, black bombers and purple hearts powered the youngsters. Rent boys serviced the upper-class hooray henrys. Hookers stood by to mop the rest up. If you couldn't feel the exhilaration, get out of the way because the teenagers craved pleasure. They weren't concerned about the war stories of their parents. Instead, they puffed their money on weed and haemorrhaged it on clothes, tunes, and a fun time. If they couldn't make it, they would Bogart it. Whatever happened, they wanted in on the action.

They cultivated their flowing locks, had sex with many partners, and sported the best clothes, grooving with the working-class bands of the day. The Who fashioned waves, and The Beatles and The Stones exploded through the capital. The once dreary, colourless boulevards of broken dreams of the wartime smoke were obliterated forever in a cloud of marijuana and music.

In 1967, six days before Ossie's 25th birthday, on the 1st of June, Ossie's friend, Peter Blake, who'd studied at the RCA, and his wife, Jann Haworth, designed the innovative record sleeve for the Beatles' eighth studio album, *Sergeant Pepper's Lonely Hearts Club Band*. It's an iconic album cover that came to define the psychedelic rock movement, and one of the most influential albums of all time, depicting seventy famous stars of the day on the front cover.

All things were possible if you stayed capable; Ossie and Celia helped garb and impress with their exquisite designs swathed over the style icons of this remarkable decade.

Michael Williams recollected in 2022 how he met Ossie at a photo shoot in South Kensington around 1967 and found him polite and cultured. Michael, a former hairdresser, modelled for Dandie Fashions for the Australian John Crittle. This became part of the peacock revolution, opening its doors in 1966 from a South Kensington mews before moving to the King's Road.

His clientele included Princess Margaret, The Beatles and The Stones. Jimi Hendrix spent the night at the store after John invited him to stay after one of the legendary parties they held there. Crittle, a heavy smoker, died in 2000, and is now buried in Australia after being deported from England in 1974.

Ossie took more trips to Paris, Spain, Ireland, and Morocco. He became an international jet-setter. He bought his first car, a Silver Buick Riviera, and drove back to Warrington for family get-togethers. The neighbours would peer through the curtains when he arrived. "Oh, Ossie must do well. Have you seen his posh car?"

In August 1967, Ossie heard the news. His friend Brian Epstein, The Beatles' manager, a Jewish boy who wore handmade shirts with gilded cufflinks, died of an accidental overdose at his London home. It was a massive blow for The Beatles, who heard of the tragedy whilst on a retreat in Bangor in North Wales. Brian, their backer, pulled the band out of Liverpool and helped them become international superstars.

The song 'You've Got to Hide Your Love Away' may have been a nod to Epstein's homosexuality. But, of course, Epstein had a massive crush on John Lennon; no matter what happened, we will never know.

They lay Brian to rest in Liverpool on August 29th, 1967. The Beatles didn't attend, but they returned for his memorial service held in London at the London Synagogue on the 17th of October, four days after John Lennon's 27th birthday. This was close by EMI studios; the Rabbi praised Brian for encouraging the band to sing about love and peace rather than hatred and war. The band left the service with tears in their eyes. Perhaps they wondered where they would go in the following career stage without him.

The death devastated Ossie. The two had been close friends. Still, the world kept onwards, and Ossie continued with his business.

When he returned to his family, he was kind and generous; they thought the world of him.

He went to New York by ship for his second Christmas. He transformed into a man with an insatiable curiosity as he headed into the new year of 1968. The Vietnam War played out to The Doors' 'Light My Fire'.

"Fashion is a form of ugliness so intolerable we have to change it every six months."

Oscar Wilde

Hippy-Ocrats

In 1968, Quorum was highlighted at the Revolution club on Bruton Place in London's Mayfair on January 25th. Ossie's shows seemed to encapsulate and embrace the vision of ultra-beauty through a lens of drug-enhanced creativity, much as if you were on a trip. Almost like a dream state, Ossie took people to places they'd never been before, entranced and in awe as they watched the show unfold.

It was a runaway success. John Lennon, Cynthia, and George looked on. Pathe newsreel was in attendance and recorded the show, which can be seen on YouTube if you wish to watch.

Ossie and Celia instigated the format for the modern-day fashion show. They converted shows into must-see social events set to music. The audience, made up of London's most fashionable and brightest stars of the day, clamoured cheek by jowl.

John Lennon told Ossie The Beatles were off to India in February to avoid all the madness. Ossie replied, "Have fun and see you when you return, darling."

Another key player who helped convey Quorum to the attention of the King's Road trio is Neil Zarach. He, in the 60s, opened premises in Fulham with his business partner Baron Alex Albrizzi. They had been to Amsterdam and spotted the potential of perspex. Although in a glass factory that sold perspex signs, the duo thought they would make magnificent tables and furniture; they imported vast quantities, and the business took off.

Alice and Ossie came into the shop and asked if they could use the premises for a fashion show. Alice and Ossie impressed Neil, and he allowed them to go ahead. There was an enormous press interest in the formidable event.

A lot of upmarket hippies came along. Some of them smoked hash. The Baron became angry and wanted them to leave, but apart from this, the show was a tremendous success. The word spread fast in the media, and everybody noticed and wanted to meet the creative trio of Alice, Ossie and Celia. Times indeed changed. Other parts of

London may not have been so wild. Still, the west London elite lived the life. Rock stars mixed with the upper classes, old Etonians and the debs with the cash to splurge on clothes and fine wines. There were parties galore all over Chelsea and Mayfair. If you were part of the in-crowd, life was a blast in the carefree, unrestricted era.

In February, The Beatles flew to Rishikesh in India. They were spiritually exhausted. Although rich and famous, they wondered what it was all for, and tried to find the answer with the Maharishi Mahesh Yogi, the leader of the Transcendental Meditation movement. The trip would be one of their most creative periods; they penned over 40 songs, many of which went on to the classic *White Album*. The trip brought a lot of media attention, and Westerners got into Indian fashion, meditation, and yoga. It was a perfect fit for the stoned hippies of the 60s who embraced the spiritual East.

They stayed at the Yogi's ashram. Amongst other Westerners who stayed there were the Scottish singer Donovan and the actress Mia Farrow. John Lennon and George Harrison got into meditation and found the peace of mind they lacked with the Beatles' frenzy.

Meanwhile, back in London, Alice's fortunes changed. Her backer, Mike Armitage, a stockbroker, realised the business was losing money and wanted to cut its losses, so they sold to Radley Gowns. The latter took on the debts in 1968 and made the business flourish again. Radley knew Ossie's significant influence was the ballet dancer Nijinsky. His love of dance encouraged his gowns to be free and fluid and not confine movement to the women who wore them.

Albert Radley was keen to promote Ossie, whom he regarded as exceptional. So they named his creations Ossie Clark for Radley and distributed them worldwide to the day's retailers. He funded large fashion shows; the first under the Clark Radley investment at the Chelsea Town Hall, where Ossie used black models for the first time. It was a spectacular triumph and made his designs obtainable to high street trade. As a result, Ossie became popular in New York and Paris.

Albert Radley remained friends with Ossie for the rest of his life; in 2002, he convinced the Victoria and Albert Museum to put up a significant exhibition of Ossie's work, which they did. It ran for ten months in July 2003, a fitting tribute for a man he'd backed for over 35 years. Albert Radley died on February 14th, 2019, at the grand old age of 94.

On September 27th, 1968, the whole of London talked about the stage production of the hippy musical *Hair* as it debuted at the Shaftesbury Theatre. It was the most controversial production to have opened for over two centuries. Anybody who was anybody had to see it. The show's stars included Paul Nicolas, Tim Curry, Ossie's good friend, Elaine Paige, Oliver Tobias and Ethel Coley, and Marsha Hunt, whom Ossie made a matching satin top and trousers for. The work broke new ground in the rock musical genre. Its profane language and on-stage nudity caused a massive sensation in the capital.

Another friend who took Ossie under his wing was the painter Patrick Procter; in 1968, they took a trip to Morocco and stayed in Marrakesh. Patrick said it was like being in the New Testament as they wandered around the bazaars. Patrick, who'd studied at the Slade and was good friends with David Hockney, whom he met in 1962 at the RCA, stood 6ft 6ins tall and wore a fez. His fingernails were painted green. He was six years older than Ossie. The two bonded over their eccentricities. Patrick painted Ossie lying on a sun lounger. David Hockney remarked years later how Ossie could be flamboyant but without the wit and polish of Procter.

In February 1969, Ossie went to see Jimi Hendrix at the Albert Hall. Jimi was glorious in a yellow tartan suit on stage. It was right next door to the RCA, where Ossie graduated four years before - he'd come a long way since then. Ossie gave up drinking Dom Perignon when the price went over £6 a bottle. Ossie first met Jimmy in New York, when he whispered in his ear, "I am a prophet from outer space and believe I won't be here very long." His words proved true. He died in the Samarkand Hotel, Lansdown Crescent, Notting Hill, on September 18th, 1970, of barbiturate intoxication.

On March 8th, 1969, the 34-year-old identical twin brothers Ronnie and Reggie Kray, the most feared and infamous gangsters in London, who had reigned over the city for the last decade, appeared at the Old Bailey in front of Justice Melford Stevenson. Although found guilty and jailed for life for the two murders of 'Jack the Hat'

McVitie and George Cornell, the judge recommended they serve a minimum of 30 years.

Ronnie said in the 60s:" The Beatles and the Stones ruled the music world. Carnaby Street and King's Road ruled the fashion world. Reg and I ruled London."

They must have felt like hollow words as they descended the steps to begin their life behind bars. The police were delighted to get these hoodlums off the city's streets. Leonard 'Nipper' Read, the Chief Superintendent of the Met's murder squad who brought the pair down, must have been smiling in the pub that night at a well-done job. He dedicated his life to bringing the Krays to justice.

In July 1969, Brian Jones of The Rolling Stones died. He was found by his Swedish girlfriend Anna Wohlin at midnight on the 2-3 July. His demise sent tremors throughout the land when he was lifeless at the bottom of his swimming pool. The month before, Brian left The Rolling Stones by mutual consent. Ossie joined The Stones for the Sympathy for the Devil Tour across America in 1969. He designed the jumpsuits for Jagger in Lycra, which could be washed in the washing machine when he came offstage.

Ossie became as famous as his clients.

The Stones were riding high, 'Honky Tonk Woman' was about to be released with a victorious homecoming gig arranged for July in London's Hyde Park. Two days after Brian's death on July 5th, 500,000 turned up to see the band play at the free concert. The band paid tribute: Jagger asked the crowd to "cool it" while he read a poem by the poet Shelley. The vast group sat silently as they heard the ode close to the Serpentine. When he finished, the guitars kicked in, and thousands of butterflies were released from cardboard boxes. The crowd went crazy. It was the first gig for their new guitarist, Mick Taylor. They played to the largest assemblage of their career so far. Although the band played out of tune, nobody seemed to mind. It celebrated Brian's brief life, dead at 27. The coroner recorded his death as drowning in fresh water and ingestion of alcohol and drugs.

A memorial gig was held on July 10th at Cheltenham Parish Church and attended by Charlie Watts and Bill Wyman. Jagger was in Australia attending Marianne Faithfull, who had tried to take her own life. Bob Dylan, his friend, paid for a silver casket.

David Hockney found a studio opposite the London Free School on Powis Terrace in Notting Hill, with its dilapidated houses and the paint peeling off the walls. It was quiet, the perfect place for him to work on his paintings. Ossie would come around when David was at work and try to entice him away, but Hockney wasn't easily led. He was happier to stay in his studio, paintbrush in hand, amongst the books and sketches littered across the room. David loved the natural light streaming through the windows on a clear day. The smell of paint and solvents gave him a regular high, and he could shut himself away from the world for weeks and concentrate on his work. Hockney had great focus when it was needed. Something deep inside him compelled him to create. He could be a workaholic. After a few hours, Ossie would take the hint and leave him to it.

Ossie flitted between Paris and New York. His life became a whirlwind of events and work. He took holidays with the Gettys in Marrakesh, where he met Yves Saint Laurent, a French designer. He was so mesmerised that he would later copy Ossie's ideas and change his shows and collections. Because of their meeting, he learned so much from the boy from the north.

In August 1969, Ossie and Celia became man and wife. Celia was pregnant with Albert and her father convinced Ossie to do the right thing and marry his daughter. The artist David Hockney was in attendance as best man, and Ossie's sister Kay was a witness. At the Kensington Registry Office, Celia wore one of Ossie's creations. Hockney suggested painting the couple as a wedding present. I'm sure they both had moments of trepidation.

That night, Ossie took Celia to the party of an Indian friend, and the next day, he flew out alone to Barbados. Hockney recalled it was a strange way to begin a marriage. Ossie felt like a prize fighter, and women fought for his attention. But although Ossie could be a quirky character, Celia still loved him and let him go. But then, the reality of marriage hit him in a big way. He would have to contemplate a mortgage, his free spirit now confined. He thought a lot on the trip and returned relaxed and happy to continue his work.

The good news came through. On October 22nd, Ossie received the fantastic information that Celia had given birth to their first child, Albert, in the Queen Charlotte's Hospital.

Whilst busy in the studio, he was thrilled to bits at the update.

Ossie loved children. He always wanted a large family and proudly took Albert out in his pram around Hyde Park to feed the ducks. Now 27 years old, he had a wife and a newborn son. Money existed in abundance.

Ossie and Celia, now as famed as their clients, headed into the new decade of 1970.

They worked well together. It was her designs that he used to construct his. Celia was hands-on and no-nonsense. Now they had a baby boy to take care of. She noticed Ossie's wild ways and hoped he might calm down now with their son to take care of.

Ossie declared himself to be an expert cutter. His glorious hero, the ballet dancer Nijinsky, inspired his clothing to free movement, not limiting the female form. "It's all in my brain and fingers. There's no one in the world to touch me." Ossie believed this, and many would agree with his reputation.

In 1970, the 60s faded; Ossie remained at the zenith of his powers. All seemed possible. He would have sensed it could only get better. His brand burned bright. Known throughout the fashion world, established without doubt, could it get any better? Albert, by now, was one year old. Celia was busy taking care of their child.

Mick Jagger starred in the film *Performance*, shot in 1968 and due to be released in August 1970. This was Mick's acting debut, and his fans waited to see him on the silver screen. The film would define the 60s in bohemian Notting Hill. The 60s saw class barriers broken down. Pop stars and gangsters, along with the aristocracy, mingled together. The film was panned by critics, but now it is regarded as a cult classic, and Jaggers's role is hailed as the most remarkable performance in an acting role by any musician.

Jagger played the reclusive rock star Turner. The film is full of drug use and sex scenes. It influenced directors Guy Richie, Martin Scorsese, and Quentin Tarantino, so it must have done its job.

Ossie loved the film, in his eyes hilarious. It featured the blonde, leggy German Italian Anita Pallenberg, who had a thing with Keith Richards, although it was rumoured she had an affair with Jagger on the set. This was also the commencement of her love affair with heroin; or perhaps it was just a rumour spread around to get people talking about the film. The film caused quite a controversy. Movie lovers still watch it today, the mark of a classic.

Ossie took a trip to Paris and drove to Germany for a fashion show in his silver Buick. On the return journey, racing back for the boat, he accidentally switched the lights off. The car bounced all over the autobahn. His friend, the machinist Kathleen Coleman, sat beside him; Ossie jumped out of the vehicle, panicking about the damage. Kathleen screamed, "Fuck the car. What about me? You could have killed us." Kathleen shook her head in anger. Ossie came to his senses and apologised

I spoke to her son, David Coleman, a car sprayer who lives in Milton Keynes after moving out of Ladbroke Grove 30 years ago. He told me his mum got dementia in 2022. He said she and Ossie had a great relationship over the years, and she spent 21 years working with Ossie and knew him better than most. Sadly, she passed away in 2022.

With his devil-may-care attitude, Ossie was always up for a laugh. In those incredible days, the last thing on his mind was to care about trivialities with money in the bank. Why shouldn't he have a fun time? He knew everybody of any consequence. He felt at the epicentre of it all. Although, at times, he could lose his temper and throw tantrums. I put a lot of it down to hiding his sexuality. It couldn't be easy suppressing his sexual desires towards men and living in the straight world, and living a lie must have always played on his mind. It is well known that men who hide their feelings have hair-trigger tempers.

He dined in Soho with Mick Jagger. He was amazed at Mick's knowledge of the back alleys of Piccadilly. The most famous rock star in the world, and Ossie was part of his inner circle of friends; he and Jagger, the Dartford-born rocker a year younger than Ossie, got on like best friends. With his star power, Mick showed off Ossie's garments and stamped his name on the map. Ossie wasn't motivated by the money. He just wanted his creations out there. Perhaps if he had been more ruthless, he could have used and abused people, but this wasn't his nature. Ossie was always entertaining company and knew how to make people laugh.

After all, nobody wanted to work with a bastard; therefore, Ossie did well in the early days. Moreover, he was fun, a breath of fresh air in an industry fraught with egos.

Mick appeared in court, happy he had only got in trouble for possession of weed, and walked away with a £200 fine on January 26th, 1970.

Fashion writer Anne Chubb remembered Ossie made the news in the *Daily Express*. He was touted as the number one fashion designer in London that year. He single-handedly began all the era's fashion trends, from maxi coats to snakeskin jackets, thirties-style crepe floating chiffon and the use of multi prints. He created the first paper J-cloth fabric. Ossie smiled when he read this aloud to Celia that morning. Still only 28, it must have been an enormous boost for his ego.

Ossie heard in July that his great friend, the Dutch-born actress, model and socialite Talitha Getty, had died in Rome, aged 30. She married John Paul Getty and was trying to get a divorce from him when she was found dead in her apartment. Talitha had been a style icon of the 60s and wore many of Ossie's creations in the era. The cause of death was alcohol and barbiturates, with rumours of heroin found in her bloodstream. She was strikingly beautiful, a tragic loss at such an early age. She'd first introduced Ossie to Yves Saint Laurent at their luxury home in Marrakesh. Ossie couldn't believe how many people died around him throughout 1970.

The Beatles released their last album in the summer of love, *Let It Be*, which climbed to number one for four weeks in June. Then, on October 4th, the legendary singer Janis Joplin, who'd electrified audiences since her debut in 1962, died of a drug overdose at 27 on the 4th of October. The rock world mourned her loss. The excesses of the 60s crept into the new decade with a vengeance.

Ossie buggered off to the Isle of Wight Festival at the end of August. He wanted to escape the Notting Hill Carnival to have a good time with nobody to stop him. With 600,000 people attending, the three-day event was headlined by the British rock band The Who, with the support of Jimi Hendrix and The Doors. What a line-up there. The event was filmed as a documentary, the *Message of Love*, a line taken from one of Hendricks's songs. Unfortunately, however, because of financial difficulties, it was only released 25 years later, in 1995.

On the other side of the pond was a young Spanish designer who went to see the editor-in-chief of *Vogue*, Diana Vreeland, with his designs in New York; she looked at his sketches and liked what she saw, especially his shoe designs. She looked him straight in the eye and said he should concentrate on the footwear. It was the spur he needed. It was Manolo Blahnik; Diana gave him Ossie's number and told him to contact the Englishman.

When the two met, Ossie invited him to design the shoes for his latest collection.

On the 10th of January 1971, after a walk outside with her friend, the most extraordinary couturier of the 20th century, 87-year-old Coco Chanel, passed away on her bed in the upmarket Hotel Ritz in Paris of a heart attack at 9pm. Her last words to her maid Celine were:" You see, this is how you die." Coco had been a familiar guest at the hotel since 1937, and she called it home.

On Wednesday, January 13th, thousands of mourners arrived at the Madeline church in Paris for her funeral. Her body was then taken and laid to rest in the Lausanne, Switzerland cemetery where she'd spent the war and she was buried in private.

Ossie said in 1971, "What's wrong with women? They don't know anything about their bodies." He wanted to design clothes for ladies to make them look like whores in the best possible taste. But, of course, he understood women and the way they moved. His eagle eyes never missed a thing. So Ossie thought of new ways to clothe them. He believed whores knew everything about their bodies, and that's why they looked so good. It was a bold but intriguing statement. Of course, this declaration offended some women. Still, many weren't offended. He encouraged them to go along with his thoughts, and indeed they did.

There is never a shortage of high or low class hookers peddling their trade in the capital. You couldn't fail to notice them unless you remained a monk or hid under a rock.

Ossie was a true pioneer. His shows electrified and hypnotised, a must-see in the capital. He placed his finger on the nation's pulse like no other designer.

Celia developed the candy flower print for Ossie and his creations. The combination of Celia's taste for bright colours and Ossie's free-flowing elegant silhouettes captured the public's imagination. Celia drew much of her inspiration from nature time and time again.

They did a string of shows. The most spectacular was held in May 1971 at the magnificent Royal Court Theatre in Sloane Square. It was a perfect venue to display their latest designs, next to the tube station at the posh end of the King's Road in the heart of Chelsea.

The audience assembled there in their multitudes. The show began in front of a brilliant star-spangled audience. Paul McCartney sat in the front row, mesmerised as the music played and the models strolled down the catwalk, with his wife, Linda. David Hockney stood in attendance. Black Magic Chocolate and Courtaulds, the fabric producers, backed the event. The aristocrats, or the hippy-ocracy of the day as they became known, were young, beautiful and stoned, and watched entranced by the spectacular cinematic show.

They juxtaposed the names Ossie, Celia and Alice with images of chocolates. They named the garments of the show after chocolates.

The packed audience gaped at the sexually charged, confrontational creations. Nipples flashed in the 70s dresses, which were inspired by the 40s. The audience roared with delight as each model sauntered by. Ossie could be glimpsed behind the curtains, scissors in one hand, cigarette in the other, always ready to help the models into the creations. Fans and clients waved at him as each model went down the runway to thunderous applause, looking like a film star from another era. Some held cards with the number of the dress worn so the clients could check their programmes. The number of each creation would tell them the price. The music was chosen to excite and exhilarate the crowd. It was pure show business as James Brown or Lou Reed blasted out. Ossie loved music, and it was always radical.

Backstage was fun, drugs on hand, and champagne corks popped when the show ended. They partied until the small hours. Ossie beamed with pleasure. It was a night to remember and went down in history in the fashion world. The problem, though, for many of the shows was that they were jammed-packed with celebrities but lacked the buyers and fashion press, which were much needed. Ossie's mind was more on performance than business. He should have had a ruthless business manager behind him. Instead, his head was in the clouds and not on the dollar.

Mick Jagger got married to the Nicaraguan-born actress Bianca Perez-Mora Macias on the French Riviera on the 12th of May 1971. The cream of rock and roll flew in by private jet - Paul McCartney, Ringo Starr, Eric Clapton, and the legendary prankster, the drummer with The Who, Keith Moon - to attend the lavish affair. The couple wore chic white suits. Ossie designed Bianca's, which hid the fact that she was four months pregnant with their daughter Jade after a whirlwind romance that led to the shotgun wedding. Mick Jagger was at the height of his powers. Every man in the country wanted to be with him as he frolicked with his wife in the Saint Tropez sunshine. Into the 1970s, Ossie's accomplishments continued to bloom. He became addicted to pleasure and was hard to hold. He went out all the time. He loved to frequent the clubs around the city like Tramps or Annabelle's; he couldn't seem to stay in.

His drug use amplified. The pop and fashion world stars pandered to him with the most refined cocaine, the best hash. As a result, he turned out more self-centred. He wanted to go to events, have extraordinary times, and party like a pop star.

He took the dangerous step of unfaithfulness to his beloved wife.

As you would expect, it hurt Celia when he slipped into the home in the wee hours while baby Albert slept close by.

Celia was an exceptional woman, fine-looking in her own right. Men were immobile and stared as she walked by. I believe Ossie was too confused and fought with his sexual individuality. He slept with women to lift his fragile self-esteem. Still, I fear his genuine interest lay in men, and he wanted to be the centre of attention. He was young. I can understand what he went through. Men have played these games worldwide, and women have suffered the consequences.

Although he loved his son - he was an affectionate and devoted father - he couldn't help himself; it would have been a constant battle to do the right thing. He was not cut out for married life. Still, Celia let him get away with it, and he would take advantage and carry on with his parties, knowing his child was cared for. He still had Celia for work, love, and encouragement.

His enthusiasm for speed and glamour wouldn't dampen throughout their marriage. Still, in their prime, they stayed together. This is because his homosexual tendencies had been so unmentionable in Warrington and Manchester's working-class environment.

Now unleashed in the carefree city of London with his close friend Mo McDermott, who didn't care what people thought about his sexual choices, Ossie must have gasped and followed suit. At last, he could be who he wanted to be. Ossie felt liberated. His reckless existence in the gay world was not beneficial to married life. However, he couldn't help himself; it must have been part of the exhilaration.

Jealousy, the oddest thoughts, and unpleasantness disturb your mind and take the joy out of any relationship. As the years rolled by, it must have ruined it for both of them. Ossie swayed from one catastrophe to another without realising where it would lead him. The thing about Ossie was that people loved him, for whatever he did was done in style. They could never accuse him of boredom.

He loved to camp things up and often did; his creative brain came up with the most outrageous ideas for dressing women. He made them slinky and straightforward. You weren't supposed to wear underwear underneath, so if the woman pulled, she could haul the dress up and have sex wherever she stood. He left a secret pocket in each garment big enough for a key and a five-pound note. He said, "It's all a young beauty would need on a night out, darling."

From his undergraduate days onwards, he was addicted to uppers, which helped him keep pace with his frantic lifestyle. But, as with most drugs, he soared skywards and came down with a bang, his head in pieces the day after a binge.

Celia described Ossie as a genius and a real artist, far better than Yves Saint Laurent. Although he lifted his cut from the 1930s, plump women could feel good in the creations. The couple catered for the well-to-do and well-dressed, and no self-respecting socialite would not be seen in their designs.

Hockney was in the progress of painting Ossie and Celia. He made sketches, took snapshots in their Notting Hill home, and worked on them in his studios. The couple were at the height of their supremacy, and the friends grew closer. Because of the size of the painting, the twosome modelled in his studios.

The name of the cat on Ossie's lap changed from Blanche to Percy, the couple's other cat. Hockney thought it sounded much better. And Percy was a slang term for penis. The cat sat on Ossie's crotch, perchance a gesture to Ossie's homosexuality. Was he bisexual or gay? He wanted children, which is one reason he married Celia in the first place, but he should have never married in hindsight.

Hockney thrashed with the painting for over a year. He amended Ossie's head over twelve times to capture the couple's unusual and intricate relationship and the strains they were going through. The painting was shortlisted for the most extraordinary picture in a poll launched by the BBC in 2005. Over 50 years later, it's so good people have been enamoured by it ever since. This painting helped cement Hockney's reputation as one of Britain's finest painters worldwide.

The masterpiece was finished in 1971. The huge canvas summarises the fashionable period Hockney believed helped contribute to the break-up of the marriage. He saw them together and may have wondered how long they would last unruffled. They were all northerners with much in common. They bounced off each other and must have had many good laughs. It was almost like a ménage à trois without sex.

Ossie valued the bohemian lifestyle. Hockney was a workhorse, and good friends with the photographer Cecil Beaton, who'd nicknamed Ossie the wizard of Oz, but Ossie, with bursts of creative energy, lacked Hockney's dedication.

They would all spend evenings together in the flat. Celia would rustle up food for the trio. They would devote the night to sketching and drawing on their pads. It could only bring them closer. They all learned much about each other. When three people become so close, it can cause difficulties. Celia treasured Hockney's friendship. She felt at ease in his company and told him everything on her mind because she trusted him.

This must have caused some unease in Ossie's mind; but if it did, he never showed it at this stage of their careers.

They were all at the top of their game; perhaps it wasn't such an issue.

Ossie sold the painting to Friends of the Tate for £7000 in 1971. Would he have sold it if he knew how much it would be worth? I don't think money drove him. He was a visionary, a rebellious artist who lived in the moment, his mind abuzz with ideas. He wanted to dress his friends in the most exquisite and sensory attire his mind could invoke. All he touched seemed to conjure up money anyhow. He must have believed there wouldn't be any problems in the future.

Ossie was invited to do a show in Paris in April, so he went out there. It became another instantaneous success and furthered his star power.

In 1972, Mr Thomas, the eccentric art teacher, invited Ossie back to Beamont Technical School in Warrington to speak to the kids.

Before he arrived, I remember Mr Thomas enriched the beige walls of Beamont Technical School. He hung Ossie's designs in the school corridors for at least a month before the great man appeared. He told us all about Ossie's star-studded career. He was known worldwide, and models and fashion houses clamoured for his dresses. He lived in London's trendy Notting Hill. He was reputed to have an extraordinary eye for the female form. The glitterati wore his garments, from The Rolling Stones to the sexy young things of the 60s who strolled down the King's Road in Chelsea. So, of course, we all became excited when we heard these stories. I remember the day he came to visit like it was yesterday.

At 13 years old, covered with spots, my hormones were everywhere. I found it hard to sit still in my wooden seat as I gazed around the audience. It electrified the school with the news that our most successful former pupil would pay a visit. The entire school sat in attendance; the floors of the assembly hall gleamed; the faint smell of polish hung in the air. The girls in the school helped make the clothes for the fashion show, inspired by Ossie's arrival and led by the sewing and craft teachers, Miss Hibbert and Mrs Carter. Girls modelled the clothes on stage. The event was to be filmed by a camera crew from *Granada Reports*.

At last, the moment we had waited for arrived. Five hundred kids scraped our chairs and craned our necks to see this global superstar who made his way towards the stage. His heels clicked as he strolled on the wooden floor dressed in a sleek white suit and an emerald green bowtie around his neck with cream and white polka dots.

How different he looked to us working-class kids. A photographer snapped away to record this momentous event. Mr Thomas greeted Ossie on the stage, wrapped arms around him, and hugged him like they were two old familiar friends.

The entire school fell silent as Mr Thomas tapped the silver head of the microphone to test if it worked. It crackled as he introduced Ossie and invited him to speak.

Ossie looked uncomfortable as he stepped over; Mr Thomas passed him the mic. In the front row, I locked my eyes on Ossie. I wondered what he would say. You could have heard a coin bounce on the floor as you waited. He opened his mouth and touched his collar-length hair. He said, "It's thanks to Mr Thomas…"

Then his voice was drowned out as the whole school erupted with laughter. Teachers Knocker Norris and Jack Atherton stifled their outburst of hilarity too. His accent sounded so feminine and gay to us youngsters.

It displeased Ossie. He dabbed his eyes with a linen handkerchief; the laughter exploded.

Ossie sprinted off the stage, followed by Mr Thomas, who tried to calm him down. They returned a few minutes later when he had composed himself. Mr Thomas brought the visit to a close. I still feel for Ossie; he must have felt humiliated. The event was shown on television later that night by *Granada Reports* to the music of 'Chantilly Lace'. They edited out the bit where Ossie loped off stage.

In many ways, Ossie stirred me. He taught me that you could be different and that there was a world outside my hometown to explore. The whole school talked about his visit for weeks afterwards, and Mr Thomas was thrilled he had been able to bring back his protégé at the height of his fame. I often wonder: my schooling was so erratic and it wasn't unusual for me to bunk out of school - it was almost a miracle I went to school on this day. If I think about it, if I had missed him, my path may have taken a different direction. So I have a lot to thank Ossie for. I will always be grateful. He made an immense impression on my teenage brain, as he did with many classmates there. I know because I have heard from those who still talk about his visit from 50 years ago. God, where does the time go?

The same year, Ossie and Celia took a two-week trip to Morocco, pregnant with their second child George, who was born on November 26th, 1972. Ossie must have been buzzing and realised how lucky he was to have this practical wife who was a fantastic mother. What more could he want?

Although known for his chiffon and crepe gowns, Ossie was a fantastic tailor. So, when Celia brought her textile designs together, they mesmerised and flattered the day's ladies. It should have been the perfect partnership. Here they were in their 30s with two beautiful children, money in the bank, their own house, and a dream come true. But cracks already appeared in the marriage. Ossie was a natural flirt. Perhaps his personality craved to be the centre of attention. It must have been hard for him to conceal his desires with all the kudos and compliments. He wanted what the world offered; the temptation was everywhere.

London had now been his home for the last ten years. The so-called rocking 60s were now behind the couple. It was time to take stock of his life so far. He had struggled with married life, perhaps, and all it encompassed. Celia stood by him for all his faults, but now she had other matters on her mind.

It's hard work with children. She must have been well miffed at Ossie's selfish streak, and Celia needed a man she could rely on. She didn't want to be his mother. Would he understand where their relationship stood if he didn't buck his ideas up? At some point, he would find out. I don't think Ossie meant any harm; he was highly sexed and couldn't control his urges. Being a notable figure and living in the sexual freedom of the 70s would go to any young man's head.

The problem was, Ossie wasn't a celebrity. He knew many, but he should have knuckled down, carried on with his work, left the parties, and gone home to his wife and kids.

In June 1972, Hawkwind released their hit record 'Silver Machine'. The band formed in Ladbroke Grove in 1969; Lemmy, who joined the band in 1971 before Motorhead, sang on the single, which reached number 3 on the UK charts.

The streets of Notting Hill were filled with such characters, who all mingled in the pubs of Portobello Road.

1973 was a spectacular year for Ossie. He'd worked with Al Radley for five years, turning the business from a £70,000 debt into a prosperous business. Ossie earned £23,000 from a percentage of sales, an eye-watering amount of money in those days. He bought a Bentley and paid a deposit for the house in Cambridge Gardens. Could life get any better?

His old friend, the Spaniard Manolo Blahnik, opened a boutique on Old Church Street in Chelsea. After that, life became hectic for the escalating star, who never forgot Ossie's help in the early days of his career. With sheer quality, the old-world charm of his footwear brought tremendous success. It became popular with the upper-crust ladies around town.

Ossie could be difficult to work with. He liked to be in charge and not have to delegate to a team; also, he hated the pressure of working to deadlines for commercial shows. From time to time, he wouldn't show up to work. He crafted works of genius but they were transient. Finally, when he showed up for work, he said, "My soul has gone into these garments, and you are treating them like dirt."

Ossie made a colossal blunder in the early days of working with Quorum. He believed Yves Saint Laurent had sent spies into the shop to duplicate his designs, and was vocal in voicing his annoyance. He offended the French designer. Because of these slurs, no French or European couture houses would work with him or sponsor his shows. This absence of money disappointed him, forcing him to sell advertising space at the events. His mouth would do him no favours; there seemed no filter on his words. He couldn't help himself. He could be his own worst enemy.

It must have been problematic for all concerned. Ossie could be rude and grumpy when the mood struck. Al Radley reiterated the importance of working in sequence and generating fresh ideas. But Ossie may have felt the pressure; instead of producing one dress, they now created 3000 garments accessible to the public at reasonable prices. Ossie may have resented this. After all, the creator perhaps thought so many products demeaned his work. No wonder they had many falling outs.

Celia felt the strain of raising the children by herself. Ossie carried on like a single man; something would have to give. I'm sure Celia felt she couldn't tolerate it if he continued for much longer.

David Hockney rented a house in Malibu from the actor Lee Marvin. Celia flew out there for a holiday and took Albert and George. Although they weren't lovers, it made Ossie angry. Celia needed a break; the holiday would be a terrific way to chill out and an excellent experience for the kids.

Hockney had moved backwards and forwards between London, LA and Paris since the late sixties. Indeed, he was making his mark on the world. Hockney was born in Bradford on the 9th of July 1937. He spent four years at the Bradford College of Art between 1953 and 1957. Because Hockney was a conscientious objector and didn't want to join the armed services, he spent his time working in hospitals to fulfil his national service. When he graduated from Bradford, he came to London in 1959 to begin his course in Art at the RCA. Again, he performed well as a student. His paintings won competitions and were bought by private collectors.

When he was a small boy, he went to the cinema with his father, which sparked his interest in Hollywood and Los Angeles. He was enamoured by the heat and light, which started his paintings of swimming pools, one of his favourite subjects.

In April, Ossie soared out to see Keith Richards in Jamaica. Then, in July, he visited Mick Jagger for his 30th birthday at Madison Square Gardens. But all this was taking its toll on his marriage; their lives drifted apart. He couldn't see it.

It was impossible to worry when caught up in the excitement of the 70s, the heady days. He wanted to have fun and to hang out with the extremely rich. Could he sustain this lifestyle if he didn't work hard on his creations? He was recognised everywhere he went.

Schoolkids chased him down the King's Road, after his autograph. He had loads of cash. Life couldn't get much more sensational. Perhaps he became addicted to fame. He would have bursts of creative energy to work like a madman and stay up all night for the latest shows. He would go on exotic jaunts and take holidays wherever the mood took him.

The eminent artists continued to create. Ossie, with a sluggish streak, was more interested in pleasure.

He made a name for himself. After years of study, he had shown determination and was driven to leave Warrington behind and chase his dreams. Only some people can do this. I'm sure his family was proud of his accomplishments. I believe he had the strength and was quite fearless. I'm sure this came from his northern working-class roots: intelligence and caustic wit.

I've no doubt he wasn't a people pleaser. He upset many without hesitation. However, folks are fascinated by guys who speak their minds and cannot back down in an argument; they can get away with murder. He would take full advantage and not think of the consequences. I'm sure he was humorous company with friends who understood his ways.

He remained his authentic self. You either liked him or lumped him. Sometimes the brightest stars shine before they burn and fade away. In 1972, his star shone and flashed across the globe. I'm sure he had a crazy sense of humour and woe betide anybody who got on his wrong side.

It attracted him to women and men; London has so much temptation. Some of the most beautiful and creative people gravitate toward this city. He must have felt like he was in a sweetshop with so much to sample and twice as many to choose from in both sexes.

We can imagine what he was like in the prime of life, hot-blooded and with little self-control. Whatever could happen? He mixed with the aristocracy and the most beautiful people on the planet, the wealthy, most recognised people. He must have wanted some of this for sure, big time.

The diaries well documented his life over the years, but I wish to learn more about the man I am trying to understand. I want to learn more insights into how the man coped, what he did, and how he thought and acted. We've got a long way to go. He is still 30 years old. I have taken walks around where he would wander the streets of the Royal Borough of Kensington and Chelsea. Along Portobello Road, down King's Road, streets often packed with pedestrians, being jolted and jarred by tourists. Through Holland Park, trying to get into his mind-set and discover more about the man. I wish to take the reader on a journey of discovery.

Ladbroke Grove is so different from fifty years ago. The buildings were run down and gloomy back in the 60s, and people would shudder if you told them you lived there. But, of course, shops change, people come and go. I've spoken to many individuals; some reminisce about the good old days, but isn't this the case in every generation? People always look back with fondness for another time. I believe in the Buddhist philosophy of living here and now and revelling in the moment. Ossie spent most of his years in West London. There is magic about Notting Hill. You feel at home here; people get along in virtual harmony more than I've ever met across the city. Notting Hill now explodes at Carnival time, a sight to behold once a year. I look forward to the celebrations. Although cancelled because of the pandemic in 2021, fingers crossed, it will happen in 2022.

With her creative flair, Celia had a brilliant eye for colour and attention to detail. She understood the day's trends. This gave Ossie the stimulus he needed to create his dresses. I cannot stress enough how important she was for Ossie's development; she was his friend long before they wed. She must have known what he was like more than anybody around him. She knew how cheeky and persuasive he could be.

Ossie wasn't the greatest of business owners. He left that side of things to others. This book is not a long list of his achievements. For further reading, you must read his diaries, which give a fascinating insight into how they worked together. Here we are in 1973, married for three years and with two young children surrounded with love. Still, Celia ran the house and took care of the children while Ossie, the man about town, partied, as we hurtle towards 1974.

"Trendy is the last stage before tacky"
Karl Lagerfeld

New York

Ossie glided into 1974, full of hope for the year ahead. Albert was four years old, and George was in his second year. However, Ossie's decadent lifestyle was driving Celia crazy by now. Ossie, being Ossie, couldn't help himself. He had to be out on the scene, like an unmarried man pogoing from party to party. Celia shook her head and wondered whether this was the man she would spend the rest of her life with.

With his free spirit, Ossie wanted to sample all the world offered. He loved walking, adored music, sketching drawings, painting and visiting galleries. A man with countless interests, he wasn't a malicious man. He could repel everything but attraction. He couldn't help himself. He was fascinated by people. He meant to do the right thing for Celia, but it was impossible for him not to have affairs with men and women. He wasn't discreet about it either.

Celia had never been a fool. He couldn't see the sadness in her eyes. It wouldn't be long before she had her say. I mean, who can blame her? Although Ossie might have been on a death wish with their relationship: he wanted the single life in town. Or did he? I don't think he knew what he wanted.

No doubt he wanted things to stay the way they stood, but this would never happen. It wouldn't be long before he regretted his ways.

Women are far more powerful when a relationship ends, especially when they have children to care for. They move on far more quickly. Millions of people regret their marriage, but at least they tried. Ossie and Celia been married for five years, which wasn't such a long time in the big scheme of things. Still, they would forever be connected through their work, the iconic painting, and, of course, their children. So here we are, still talking about their relationship. It must amuse Celia somehow, or maybe it irritates her after all these years. She is still producing and got on with her life, and good luck.

The marriage crumbled in 1974. Ossie wasn't in a suitable headspace. He went to New York and partied with Andy Warhol, who'd suggested that in 1968, everybody would have their fifteen minutes of fame. Warhol made his name in the pop art movement in the 60s. Ossie jumped headfirst into the drug-fuelled nightlife. With the likes of Gary Glitter and Brian Ferry, he hit the dance floors and the bars. His drug consumption rocketed. Celia let him do his thing. But the one thing that did her head in was his fling with Johnny Dewe Matthis, whom he knew from the late 60s.

No woman in their right mind would put up with such nonsense. He drove her into the arms of another man: she had a brief affair with the painter Adrian George. It left Ossie devastated. David Hockney stepped in and gave Celia comfort. I'm sure Ossie got the hump. But there would always be losers when you took sides.

He felt anger towards Hockney, and no doubt harboured it for the rest of his life. They say time is a great healer, but this is not always the case.

Ossie began a diary in 1974 at the suggestion of his psychiatrist. He wrote 30 pages in a stream-of-consciousness style, filling in the gaps of his early years growing up in Warrington. Although the start of the year was hectic and fast-paced, Ossie ended the year with the wreckage of his wife and sons gone for good.

Still, he went out and partied and did what single men do when they are alone a lot of the time, strung out like a laboratory ape, which gave him delusions of grandeur. He sought out sex with casual strangers.

Ossie ran with the rock stars, hippy-ocracy, and beautiful models who hung out in the city. He drank far too much and took an abundance of drugs, and who could blame him? It helped to mask the agony he must have felt. Maybe the glamour didn't seem so glamorous.

They say it can take three years to get over any split. Still, when you have a drink in your hand and drugs in your nose, surrounded by gorgeous men and women, you have fun and try to forget your troubles till you wake up with a stranger who couldn't care less about you. Life can be brutal and full of twists and turns for all of us.

He moved into a flat on Powis Terrace and realised his Jekyll and Hyde personality. The arguments became more furious between him and Celia. He said David Hockney had meddled in their business and wished he would stay out of it and concentrate on his art.

Life became hard for Ossie; his emotions were manic. He wanted to stay with the children, but Celia wasn't interested. He would have cocaine splurges, which lasted for weeks afterwards; he would be remorseful, clean his flat, and make the meals. Then he'd go around seeing Celia take the children out. He hurt in a big way.

Ossie wanted to appreciate his boys. So he went to the flat in Linden Gardens, where Celia lived with their sons. He went down with suicidal thoughts. What was life all about, all alone without the children?

Celia allowed him to see the boys. They would go to London Zoo or the galleries.

On October 14th, he came unstuck. After picking Albert up at the school gates, he was pulled over by the police and arrested for drunk driving. He was brought to Notting Hill police station and gave a blood sample.

Celia exploded with anger and told him not to see the boys daily; twice a week and weekends were enough. Perhaps Ossie thought Celia was heavy-handed, but she wanted to protect their sons.

The next day, Ossie saw Alice with his lawyer about the driving charge and, like a fool, drank more vodka. His head was all over the place with his stupidity from the day before. The lawyer spoke about the law and the consequences. Ossie drank more through the night. He'd found out about Celia's affair. He became furious and jumped into a cab like a lunatic to get over to Linden Gardens. He wasn't in the right frame of mind, angry and jealous. When Celia wrenched the door open, Ossie flew at her, making accusations. He kicked her, lashed out, and broke her nose. Blood gushed across her face. Ossie wrote this in his diaries. Celia rushed to the phone sobbing and called the police, and they ushered him off the premises.

The next day, he woke up with a massive hangover, wracked with guilt. He knew how much of a mess of their married life he had brought on himself. His affairs and betrayals pushed Celia away. He must have felt like shit about his actions. He found out Celia had taken an injunction out on him to stop him from coming to Linden Gardens. It was much harder to see the boys because of his madness.

Who could blame Celia? She would have been so hurt in more ways than one.

Life is never easy to understand. I doubt Celia could bring herself to forgive him so soon after the incident. She must have been in a terrible state and wanted nothing to do with him. But the tragedy of breakups never ends well; they were passionate, creative people and tempers flared.

Ossie was in a sad state of mind the next day. A couple of days later, he drove to Paris. It took his mind off the damage he'd caused. There could be nothing worse than lying in a room alone when you've done wrong and you know it. David Hockney repeatedly warned him to be calm about his relations with Celia. He wished he'd paid heed now. He thought about going to court to claim custody of the boys, but he knew that this wasn't reasonable. Still, he would always be there for them, without a doubt, and he wouldn't give up without a fight.

He came back from Paris in a depressed state. He wanted to write a letter to Celia and win her back; he knew it was futile. On October 27th, Albert's birthday, they appeared in the Law Courts of the Strand and the judge dissolved the marriage. Ossie was single; the thought horrified him. He was alone, without the children.

On November 30th, he soared out to Hong Kong for two weeks with Al Radley, who'd arranged to meet fashion buyers there. Ossie wasn't in any state to do business. Celia had driven him to the airport with the children and dropped him off. There must have been times when they both knew they'd been friends, whatever the marital outcome.

On December 1st, he arrived in Hong Kong. He couldn't stop thinking about the kids everywhere he went. He noticed mothers with prams. The reminders were so painful. He felt alone and alienated in his modern hotel room. He thought about returning to London, but what would be there for him, in a big house by himself?

He attended none of the meetings. Instead, every song he heard on the radio reminded him of what he'd lost with Celia. Will I ever get over this? What will my life be like now? Where will my career go from here? He had many doubts and worries in his mind.

So he walked the streets of Hong Kong, his mind in a constant state of agitation.

On the 8th of December, he rang Celia to check up on the children. It was good to hear her voice; it comforted him. Still, Celia didn't want to give him any false hope, and she told him Albert had suffered from measles, and his beautiful RCA dress had been stolen. Celia hung up, leaving Ossie once again heartbroken. I think she did the right thing rather than make him believe things could work out in the future. Sometimes you must be cruel to be kind. This was one of those times.

Anyone who's been through a divorce can relate to this. He lay in his hotel room and read books to take his mind off things. He bought presents for the children and looked forward to getting these two weeks over and returning to London.

A *Hong Kong Standard* write-up about his life and achievement in the newspaper gave him a slight boost. They appreciated his work in the Far East.

The next day, he flew back to London, and went to see Celia a few days later. Again, he begged, "I love you. I need you to take me back."

Celia wasn't interested; she said no; she had made her mind up. Ossie got down on his knees. He records in his diary his grovels, the act of a desperate man who knew he only had himself to blame. Still, he was determined to try. You don't give up without trying, he reasoned with himself.

The film *A Bigger Splash* was released in 1974. It was centred on David Hockney and his friends in Notting Hill. Celia was in the film, and it captured pivotal moments in their lives over the last couple of years. The film crew bagged a 1972 Ossie/Celia show and the after-party of the Miss World alternative, the anti-beauty spectacle. There was an almost dream-like quality to the filming. If you have not yet seen it, take the time to watch it and transport yourself back to the era.

"The best things in life are free. The second best is very expensive"

Coco Chanel

Percy Savage

I chatted with the diminutive and well-spoken Highgate artist Beverley Issacs, a friend whom I met through Rainbow George, the eccentric leader of the Rainbow Party (who appointed her the Mini-Star of Colours), at her studio filled with exquisite paintings. Some are waiting to be completed, with paint tubes, photographs and hardcover-lined walls. She reminded me about an extraordinary man, who should be mentioned, in European fashion. Beverly hung out with him around Camden's pubs and art galleries before he died, when they lived there in the early noughties. She recalled his hilarious company, with many stories of his time in couture.

In 1974, the 6ft-3 legendary 48-year-old Percy Savage flew to London from Paris and moved into a house in Camden Town. He waltzed around the city in his trademark black fedora, shrouded in cigarette smoke from his favourite Gauloise cigarettes. Savage was an Australian fashion publicist, designer, artist, and raconteur. He left Australia as a 20-year-old and spent the rest of his life living and working in Europe. He was the first to be employed in a public relations capacity in haute couture. He wanted to come to London and put on a show at the London Ritz, followed by his London collections in 1978, the precursor to London Fashion Week. Savage held great sway in the world of fashion: he was the man who elevated Yves Saint Laurent and the house of Lanvin.

He met Ossie at a party in the Ritz, the two got on well, and Ossie learned much from fashion's elder statesman. It was rumoured that when Savage travelled for the House of Dior to source fur, Emperor Haile Selassie had gifted him two cheetahs, and Percy would walk them on leads around the Bois de Boulogne.

Savage set sail to London in 1947 to study on a Commonwealth scholarship at the Slade Art School and stayed only two weeks. After that, he couldn't stand the gloomy grey capital and made haste to Paris. He met the French writer Jean Cocteau and moved with the crème of Parisian society. Cocteau influenced Percy's work, and the two became firm friends. When he was a 15-year-old boy in Australia, he was bitten by a poisonous adder on his finger. Percy at once chopped it off with a sharpened hoe; the pain must have been unbearable, but the boy's quick thinking saved his life. Cocteau would later use this as his inspiration for the painting he did of Savage, The Angel Has Three Fingers. After he graduated in History and Art at the Sorbonne in Paris, he worked with the House of Lanvin. He designed silk scarves for the fashion house. Then, in 1951, he was asked to become the press officer for the newly formed press office of Lanvin for the next ten years. Again, he made his work a success and made connections throughout Europe. He was a man to know; he did all the behind-the-scenes jobs.

He had an expense account to entertain clients. He courted such figures as Greta Garbo and Jackie Kennedy. He underlined the importance of this new sort of PR after the war. Savage was the first to see the value of celebrities wearing designer clothes at gala events. When actress Elizabeth Taylor arrived in Paris in 1954, he overturned the established order of fashion promotion by circumventing a well-respected law issued by the French Ministry of Culture, which banned fashion houses from advertising their clothes in the media. Savage went to the Hotel Meurice and convinced Elizabeth Taylor to wear a Lanvin dress to a film premiere that night. After she promised him she would, Savage alerted the French press. When the press asked her where the dress came from, she said it was "From Lanvin; isn't it divine?" The publicity it gained was massive, and as a result, the ban was dropped.

Savage later said PR was essential and cost less than an advertising budget. For the price of a couple of free lunches, you could get the same amount of publicity in *The Times* or *The Telegraph*. The perfume Eau Sauvage was named after Percy by Christian Dior after Percy became a great friend of the designer. Savage recalled being invited to Christian's house for a brainstorming session to name a new perfume and arriving late. Somebody banged on the table. "Oh, Savage, you are always late." Dior clapped his hands and said, "That's it, Eau Sauvage." Savage introduced the young Yves Saint Laurent to Dior. Percy recommended that Dior "take the boy on and give him employment." Dior heeded this advice, and Yves Saint Laurent became one of the world's most famous fashion designers. Percy also introduced Mary Quant to the American press and made her a global superstar.

When he arrived back in London, he made it his life's work to elevate the profile of British fashion. His years at the forefront of PR helped boost the profile of Bruce Oldfield, Vivienne Westwood, Katharine Hamnett, Zandra Rhodes and, of course, Ossie Clark. He had a dynamism to be reckoned with and there was nothing he didn't know about fashion. With his gilt-edged credentials for PR, he knew how to manipulate the media and became an essential asset to the London fashion world. He deserves to have a book written on his life and experiences in his own right.

" The joy of dressing is an art."
John Galliano

Juno Gemes

An untrue article stating that Celia had left Ossie for David Hockney appeared in the newspapers. Ossie couldn't bear the thought of them together, although they were friends and never lovers. His head was in bits. He couldn't stop thinking about Celia and the boys. His mother wrote him a Christmas card and said Christmas meant nothing without children, which added to his fragile state of mind. He rang Celia and begged her to spend time together for Christmas with the children, but she refused.

Ossie spent the Christmas of 1974 alone in the house in Cambridge Gardens, which he had bought when he sold the David Hockney painting. He tried to get Celia to move in because the place was spacious. However, Celia had never been interested.

All the things in the world he could have had have now gutted him. The man wanted his wife and children with him. He was in total despair. The break-up of any relationship is never easy and when there are children involved, it only doubles the pain. He had many thoughts of suicide, whether honest or imagined. For sure, he went through a major depression.

Let's face it; he had a right to be down. Still, he had his sense of humour and creativity, and 1975 would soon be here.

Ossie became a bit more optimistic now, with 1974 out of the way. For sure, it couldn't get any worse. With a roof over his head, somewhere, he could gather his thoughts to work out what to do. He knew he must get on with his life. At thirty-three years of age, he wasn't an old man. Things could change in the blink of an eye and often do.

He threw dinner get-togethers for parties of ten. He became an excellent cook and a witty and entertaining host. He tidied the house and garden, planted flowers and shrubs, and turned the house into a home. Ossie and Celia had known each other for 14 years. Ok, they were divorced, but they could be friends.

He loved to work in the garden and took to reading great literature. The highlight of his life would be when he saw the children for the weekend every two weeks. Although he had money concerns on his mind, he kept these thoughts to himself. He realised he must sell his Bentley to help his finances. He took a trip to Al Radley and negotiated a new contract. Everybody who wore Ossie's creations felt like a star and knew they would have a fantastic night out. This was how the dresses made people think. Al still had great faith in Ossie.

Celia had cash troubles, and she would chase money up from Ossie. She still needed to pay the rent for the Linden Gardens flat; Ossie helped where he could. He was never mean with his money, which was part of his problem. Instead, he gave what he could and helped support the children, which added to his financial woes.

Celia took full responsibility for the children, though of course, Ossie wanted them to live with him. But was he being realistic? Of course, he loved them, and I am sure he would have done his best. Life is full of difficulties, but the main thing is keeping employed, creating, and bringing the money in.

Still, he always had time for his friends. Juno Gemes, the Australian multi-media artist and photographer, gave me a story about Ossie that showed his generosity. She recalled a time in 1975:

"I lived in Ballantyne Street in a house shared with the beautiful Henrietta Partridge, Mark Palmer, Nicholas Gormonston and Roderick O'Connor.

"Yes, all the members of our household were beautiful. But, likewise, the entire street was inhabited by lovely people - inside and out. A short walk to Ossie and Celia Birtwell's magic shop. Henrietta and I found our way to it often. We loved wearing his dreamy clothes in crepe de Chine and other marvellous soft floaty fabrics. More than anyone else, any other designer in Chelsea, Ossie based many designs on the glamorous shapes of 1930s design. He was a genius pattern maker—his delicate fabrics with Celia's exquisite prints, and the inventive cut of the materials made for the dreamiest and most sexy clothes in Chelsea. And that's calling it. I told him so. One felt marvellous in his clothes. Cool and sexy.

"What people may not know is how kind Ozzie could be.

"Pregnant with my son Orlando, I chose to have him alone. It was a decision made in the early days of second-wave feminism. Many dear friends warned me this was just too hard a choice - of course, they were right.

"Around late January 1975, I went to lunch with David Litvanoff on the King's Road when Nicky Samuels-Waymouth swept in to join us. She announced that she was about to get married again, this time to NY jeweller Ken Lane on Feb 18, and Christopher Gibbs would throw a marvellous wedding party for her at his house on Cheyenne Walk - we must promise at once to come. We promised. But what to wear? I was due by this time. With this question in mind, I went to visit Ossie. He commiserated with humour and warmth and suggested I try on the most divine silk chiffon, black gipsy dress with Celia's red and green hand-blocked flowers printed on it. It had swirls of fabric draped around my body - so my baby bump was visible. This dress stayed perfect, and it felt divine when I wore it. Only one problem - I couldn't afford it.

"I explained this to Ozzie, who insisted I take the dress free. And he maintained that I keep it. So I went to the party. I am well-dressed at Nicky's and Christopher's with all our tribe. And the notable figures of our time present - I remember I almost fell over David Frost.

"Nigel Waymouth suggested I should give birth at once at the party - as this would make the occasion more memorable. He plied me with champagne and sweet hashish to help me along. I had only to walk a small way home; just as my water broke at 5am on the 19th of February - I rang Georgie Downs and Bill. They drove me across London at dawn to Middlesex Hospital for the birth of my son Orlando. Georgie, Judy Ahern and my mother, Lucy Gemes, were also present on this joyful occasion.

"I was thankful to Nigel and felt safe with my marvellous tribe of supporters.

"The dress is still with me. I will always be grateful to Ossie and remember him with the greatest affection. Such a lithe, charming spirit with a light touch and quick wit. An adorable genius among our brilliant tribe in Chelsea."

I love to hear these stories about Ossie. His life was a whirlwind, and he overcame his difficulties, but it showed what a wonderful man he could be. I believe he was one of life's characters and we shouldn't judge him. He seemed to move quickly in and out of the doors of the London elite. Whether it be a mansion in the country or a book-lined elegant pad in Chelsea, he was more than welcome in the 70s, it seemed.

His talent and force of personality enamoured and enraged; a strange, dangerous mix of wit and charisma that was hard to contain.

Ossie's friend, the outrageous Quentin Crisp, was another Chelsea wit from the tribe. His autobiography *The Naked Civil Servant* turned him into a star when the actor John Hurt played him on television. It aired in the UK and US in 1975. Immortalised by Sting's 'Englishman in New York', Quentin moved to New York to capitalise on his fame.

In January 1976, Ossie was busted for cannabis possession and speed. He pleaded guilty. It wasn't the crime of the century - and let's face it, who wasn't smoking hash and doing a bit of speed in the 70s? The cells were full of bright young men, articulate and well-dressed, who loved drugs; LSD and hash were the norm. The magistrates were lenient and gave him a fine of £70; he was more pissed off that the police confiscated his drugs and he would have had to go out and replenish the stock again.

It had now been over two years since the divorce from Celia. He was trying to get on with his life. However, he felt a massive loss.

Celia left the fashion industry to concentrate on the boys and give them her full attention. First, she did part-time work at colleges around London. Then her friend David Hockney persuaded her to be a life model to bring money in. With much in common and a love for Paris, Celia and Hockney watched old Laurel and Hardy films together. They were both from the north with influential mothers, and they made each other laugh, a sure sign of genuine friendship. They drew a lot closer to each other as the years went by.

This strained the relationship with Ossie, who felt he was being pushed out of the picture. Meanwhile, depression kicked in. Sometimes he would struggle to get out of bed without a joint or a drink to lift his mood, like countless others in the same position. But life is murky and grey when things go wrong.

The divorce had a massive impact on his life, but it made him realise he had brought it on himself. Ossie knew he had a big ego at the time of his fame and struggled with his married life. After the divorce, he neglected his work, making his business unreliable over the next few years. He sometimes wrecked his head with drink and drugs, which shattered his motivation, but soon he would have to get it together and regain his mojo.

So, as he moved toward the long red-hot summer of 1976, Ossie had plenty of time to think things over as he worked on his garden. And his ambition surfaced again. He knew he must get out of the melancholy and get his life back on track. He had his children to support. This would have been a constant worry on his mind. Ossie would never have wanted them to go without if he could help it. He knew the kids were in safe hands with Celia, but it would affect his pride if he couldn't contribute. They were the illuminations of his life and one of the main reasons he would snap out of it and focus again on his work.

Over this summer, the black teenagers at Notting Hill Carnival clashed with the police on the streets. It was believed a pickpocket was arrested as he moved sneakily through the crowd on Portobello Road, and black youths came to his aid. There were about 150,000 people at the event. Young Clash members were present, which inspired them to write the song 'White Riot' as a call out to the white people to protest with the same uproar.

Over in Chelsea, an innovative new designer on the King's Road burst out, to some extent taking the spotlight from Ossie's garments. The imaginative Malcolm McLaren was the mouthpiece for Vivienne Westwood and her designs. They opened the shop in 1971 and named it Let it Rock, wanting to eliminate the hippy fashions of the 60s. They came out with a much more aggressive style on the King's Road. Vivienne had met Malcolm in 1965 when still a bit of a Dolly Daydream; Malcolm came from a family of Jewish rag trade merchants who knew about art, politics and culture. Malcolm introduced her to all these things, and the relationship flourished.

The shop went through numerous incarnations. In 1973, they called it Too Fast to Live and Too Young to Die. They renamed it Sex, selling bondage clothing, the following year; they set out to provoke. In '76, they called it Seditionaries, and they grabbed all the attention in the media with the band The Sex Pistols. With their swagger and the way they dressed, times moved fast. The kids on the street gravitated towards their shop and wanted something new. The Sex Pistols were more than ready to give it to them. Anti-establishment, punk became fashionable. Unique and fresh, it left an indelible mark on the country's youth.

McLaren, an ideas man, formed the band to sell his t-shirts. Music sold fashion, and he jumped in with both feet. Nothing was too scandalous in his book—the more significant the surprise, the better the impact.

The country pogoed to 'Anarchy in the UK'. It was released in November 1976, and things would never be the same.

Ossie couldn't fail to notice. He had an uneasy admiration for what punk represented. At least they weren't drab and brought colour into people's lives.

However, he would soon go out of favour with the cost of his garments. The kids moved on, and the King's Road changed after they took over.

Ossie would feel down, but he never failed to keep in touch with his northern roots, ringing his mother. Sometimes he would jump in his car to visit her on a whim. Getting out of London and driving the 200 miles back to see the family always cheered him up and gave him the strength and motivation to spring back into action. It was an escape from city life and a great way to reconnect and forget his worries, if only for a short time.

"Fashion should be a form of escapism and not a form of imprisonment."
Alexander McQueen

Rivals

In January 1977, the community of Chelsea was energetic with originality; a new star arrived from Jamaica and brought his entourage with him. Robert Nestor Marley fled Jamaica, moved into the area, and rented a flat on Oakley Street close to the action. The weed dealers were soon banging on his door.

In the meantime, Ossie's four-year contract with Quorum and Radley ended. Still, he had the acumen to take on a new business partner, Peter Jones, and a manager, Tony Calder, who'd worked for The Stones 'manager Andrew Oldham, and set up Ossie Clark Ltd. Tony and Peter invested their money into the business and opened premises at 117a Fulham Road. It looked like things were going up for Ossie again, and it felt good. Ossie put his re-emergence down to the manageress of the shop, Sheila Oldham, the former wife of Andrew, The Stones' manager. She urged Ossie to see an acupuncturist, and he spent the next four months having sessions.

It seemed to do the trick. His depression lifted, and his mood changed. At last, he felt on top of the world, more than ready to climb back from the bottom of the pit and happy to be alive and back in action.

Ossie relished the revival. His shows were hits, and he got rave reviews from the press.

His rival Malcolm McLaren and The Sex Pistols released their second single in the summer of 1977, 'God Save the Queen', to coincide with the Queen's silver 25th anniversary. It was a stroke of genius by McLaren. Or was it luck? Whatever the way, it helped them. It caused so much controversy that the BBC refused to play it, and Woolworths wouldn't sell it in any shops. However, the publicity the band reaped became immense and it is still considered one of the most incredible publicity stunts ever.

'God Save the Queen' exploded in the UK, sold over 150,000 copies daily, and reached number 2 behind Rod Stewart's 'I Don't Want to Talk About It'.

One week after 'God Save the Queen' was released, radio stations refused to play it. So Malcolm borrowed a boat from the entrepreneur Richard Branson and sailed up the Thames with The Sex Pistols to regale the Queen as they passed the Houses of Parliament. The band performed 'Anarchy in the UK' and 'God Save the Queen'.

The police were enraged, seized the boat, and blamed McLaren. They hauled him off the boat and threw him in a Black Maria. As they went to slam it shut Malcolm shouted "You are fucking fascist bastards!" He knew the publicity was priceless; I'm sure he laughed at the police station.

Johnny Rotten couldn't stand Malcolm. They were like chalk and cheese; still, they needed each other at first.

Although they paid for the privilege, the Sex Pistols wore Vivian's creations, which didn't go down too well with the band, especially Johnny, who found her clothes restrictive when he wore them. I don't think they liked each other. They had a clash of personalities, both being headstrong and opinionated.

The Sex Pistols went on their ill-fated tour of America in January 1978. Sid Vicious the bassist was strung out on heroin. Lead singer Johnny Rotten barely spoke to his bandmates. McLaren booked them to play a string of redneck bars across the deep south, a terrible idea. The crowd was composed of hippies on their last night of the 12-day tour at San Francisco's Winterland Ballroom. The sound man didn't know his job. After singing, Johnny shouted, "Ever get the feeling you've been cheated on?" He dropped the mic and walked off stage; it would be the last time the band played together until 18 years later, in 1996. In May 2022, the six-part series on the Sex Pistols was released, directed by Danny Boyle, based on the book by Steve Jones, *Lonely Boy*. Johnny Rotten objected and called it a middle-class fantasy but failed to get the series stopped in court.

Meanwhile, Ossie frequented a gay club on High Street, Kensington, then called Yours and Mine, later renamed the Sombrero Club. El Sombrero was a restaurant with the club in the basement below; the customers hustled and smooched together. A Mexican hat lit up in neon flashed outside.

Now divorced, Ossie could be himself. Surrounded by the gay world, he didn't need to worry about other people's thoughts.

I know he loved a good time and wanted to celebrate his success after the last few years. He deserved to have some fun. This was the environment he needed to be in. People may wonder about Ossie's temper; he had a speedy wit, and an expertise with one-liners, which could unsettle you if you weren't used to his sense of humour and took offence. He could mix with anybody from the bohemians of Notting Hill to the aristocracy and upper-crust dandies of Chelsea; nothing seemed to faze him.

Many people thought he was gay long before he married Celia. His dreadful eruptions were a mechanism for Ossie and he was never scared of reactions. He was intelligent and ultra-sharp. Have you tried to pick on a gay man? They will come right back at you and shoot you down in flames before you can think of an answer. He wasn't put off by some mouthy Neanderthal. Instead, he developed a cheeky riposte for any occasion. This continued throughout his life.

He wasn't an arse licker. He was a rebel who turned out masterpieces. When the seasons changed every six months, he was under immense pressure. His love of drugs and a good time clouded his judgment. His talent could go to waste. It wasn't Celia's fault. It wasn't Ossie's fault; it happened. It all became a bit too much.

He knew life was short. He took drugs to forget and to have fun. He loved the hedonistic lifestyle, and why not? Not everybody is cut out for the 9 to 5 lifestyle, married with a mortgage.

He was free of all this now, so he sought something to ease his melancholy and get back into life. After all, he was a man with a lot to offer, with a lot of experience behind him. He wanted to find somebody who could stimulate him to have conversations with. He had been on his own for the last five years. A man can get lonely. No matter who you are, gay or straight, we all want to feel a connection with somebody in this world. Ossie found it in the gay world.

Yes, of course, he had been used to the good life back in the 60s, and who wouldn't be pissed off if you found yourself skint and back in obscurity? Still, it develops your character; it makes you who you are. So he didn't fall by the wayside. Instead, he came down to earth with the rest of us, and his love of music and the gay world went hand in hand.

I'm sure he networked; in the back of his mind, you had to be out to connect: if you stayed home, nothing would happen. When you are out having a good time, your worries are pushed to the back of your mind, at least for that night. Yes, it can be a vicious circle of drink and drugs. Ossie took them for the pure fun and escapism they brought. Some enjoy drugs once a month. Some are at it every night, which can harm your mental health.

Ossie poured his heart and soul into the industry throughout his fashion career. Still, you are only as good as your last collection. It had been a while since Ossie's last collection, so he needed to relieve the pressure and find some outlet for this creative energy that seemed to come and go in waves of madness.

However, the world of fun was out there. You didn't need to be a multi-millionaire to go to the Sombrero. Ossie jumped in headfirst and went for it. He was lonesome, hankering after somebody to cater to his emotional needs, and stimulate his mind. Ossie met the next love of his life in January 1978, a 19-year-old waiter, Nick Balaban. Ossie flirted with him and became a regular customer, working his charisma on the boy over the months.

Nick had fallen in love with Hockney's painting of Mr and Mrs Clarke before meeting Ossie. It would have flattered him when he found out who Ossie was. A man of Ossie's repute would be a great catch, so the pair dated; Ossie fell for Nick big time, and after his sons, Albert and George, Nick would be the next great love in his life.

Ossie, at 35 years of age, was 16 years older than Nick. He wanted to inform him about life and take him under his wing. He needed somebody to love and care for. Whether they slept together the first couple of years - because Nick legally had to wait until he was 21 - is anybody's guess. Still, I'm sure this was the least of their worries. They were in love and wanted to know each other. At least the start of a fresh romance is always heady in the honeymoon period.

Ossie loved the music, and in the Sombrero, an attention-grabbing gay club, the music pumped out the 70s vibe, funky and soulful. The dance floor was like something out of *Saturday Night*

Fever. You felt like somebody when you came down the spiral staircase and hit the multi-coloured dance floor, which resembled a boxing ring. They served food to get a late licence: a piece of ham and salad on a paper plate the customers never ate, but it kept the council and the police happy. The club opened in the 60s and went through various incarnations, as clubs do, to keep it exciting and fresh.

It was a twenty-minute walk for Ossie, and the quickest way was to cut through Holland Walk, lined with guys looking for some fun and games. It wasn't unusual for guys to touch guys up hundreds of times in the club. The gay world is nothing like the straight world. They were out to party and played the best music; people wanted to go to because they heard how much fun you could have.

Ossie loved to dance. He would be spotted on the dance floor under the strobe lights. Sombrero was often packed; David Bowie, Freddie Mercury, Boy George, and Johnny Rotten went there. The American Lee Black Childers, the manager of the Heartbreakers and good friend of Andy Warhol, loved it there. He once said to Ossie, "I can never understand these English kids who go home and tell their parents they are gay. Hell, they should come and tell me; I know where all the best gay clubs in New York are." Ossie rolled his eyes in amusement.

The heterosexual lead singer of the cult underground band, the London Cowboys, Steve Dior, whose parents owned a hotel off High Street Kensington, went there. Steve is famed for introducing Nancy Spungen to Sid Vicious. We all know where that led. So many punks would go to the club. It was a crazy night there and a place to have fun.

The crowd was a mix of Asian and European queens with gold chains, hairspray, and clutch bags. Older men paraded their young lovers on the dance floor. Transvestites ran riot, and men in drag dressed as 40s divas added to the intoxicated ambience; people flocked there from all over London. It was one of the best gay clubs in London.

Also popular was the gay club Louie's in Earls Court, The Phoenix in Oxford Street, and Heaven in Charring Cross. London buzzed if you were young and gay and wanted some action. Many older guys welcomed you with open arms and smiles, plied you with drinks and promises. Kids were off their heads and on the dance floors with a small brown bottle of amyl nitrate, or poppers, as they became known. Tucked in a sweaty palm, as soon as you shook the bottle with all your might, unscrewed the top, and stuck the bottle under your nose, you snorted the liquid vapours and they gave you such an intense rush you thought you could explode. It made you dance like crazy and fuck like a demon.

The gay clubs were great for straight guys, too. There was a laid-back atmosphere, and everybody knew loads of girls hung around the gay guys, and if you copped lucky with one for a one-night stand, the wilder the sex, the better. It didn't take long for a place to be rammed out. Shallow conversations with superficial sex were de rigueur. No one stood around looking cool. Instead, you hit the dance floor, animated with good quality coke and cocktails, or if you were skint, you could steal a drink from a stranger's table - what they called mine sweeping back in my day. It was a carefree, decadent world where you could indulge your illusions before the Aids pandemic came along six years later.

Ossie gave a two-page interview with the *Chelsea Scoop*, a British underground fashion magazine co-founded by Charlie Tenant, who also edited the publication in the same year. Charlie, the son of Colin Tennant or Baron Glenconner, bought the island of Mustique, where Princess Margaret loved to stay. After meeting Andy Warhol, Charlie returned from New York to launch the magazine.

In this issue was an interview with another gay legend, the incomparable Quentin Crisp, a colourful homosexual who spent time as a rent boy in his teenage years. He was now a life model who wore outlandish clothing, dyed his hair purple and painted his fingernails. He amused some and drew threats of violence from others. He would be seen mincing down the Kings Road to one of his life modelling classes. He lived in the same flat for 40 years, which Quentin claimed he never cleaned:" Oh darling, after four years, the dust gets no worse." His waspish wit drew people to him.

This is a scarce magazine. There were merely two publications. It is now on eBay for £650, a rare collector's item.

Not long afterwards, Ossie flew to New York. At one show, he demanded courtesy. He wanted to be centre stage, told people to fuck off, and pouted if he didn't get what he wanted. He didn't realise times had moved on. His ten years of fame had ended. This must have driven him mad. People remarked how much of a pain in the arse he had become. He was still a face, but not in quite the same way as he had been in the earlier decade.

When he flew back to London, and the months flashed by in the summer, Ossie found he couldn't afford his mortgage payments. The house in Cambridge Gardens was repossessed. This brought back his depression. All the things he had worked hard for were taken away by the receivers; it was a massive blow in any man's life. They forced him out onto the streets, but Mariane Faithfull rented him a basement flat in Chelsea, as luck would have it. It was, however, only temporary.

He'd got his life together after the split from Celia; but the business, Ossie Clark Ltd, wasn't making any money. Ossie still worked with Celia. They couldn't understand why the company was failing.

Still, he had to get on with his life, and what doesn't kill you can get you back in the game.

By the end of 1978, he would have to take stock and get his life back.

Ossie was in love with Nick and persuaded him to move into the flat in Chelsea. He thought Nick showed promise because he was interested in art and fashion. He recommended that Nick apply to the Byam Shaw School of Art, which specialised in fine art, and offered foundation and degree-level courses. Ossie thought he should go for it and not hang around; Nick needed the spur to push him in the right direction. Nick announced he'd applied for an interview with the school. Now it was a waiting game to see when they would respond. He wasn't sure if they would accept him; fingers crossed, he said to Ossie.

Marianne began recording an album with her then-boyfriend, punk musician Ben Brierly. The house they shared was nothing like Ossie's former home in Cambridge Gardens. Instead, it was a house full of rock and roll and decadence. Ossie captured Marianne's attention. She contemplated a threesome but knew the sorrow it would cause.

Marianne and Ossie were fascinated by each other; they were both powerful characters and loved to have fun. Of course, they bounced off each other. Ossie, now openly gay, still oozed magnetism that pleased both sexes. You could never say never in Ossie's world. His mind was receptive to all kinds. Marianne brought out the fun in Ossie, and he needed this after the problems he'd been through.

Ossie was invited to parties, and he went to the wedding of the rock god Eric Clapton and Patti Boyd. He went there with Chelita Secunda, who recalled it was the wedding of the year, dominated by the best musicians.

Ossie became aware that he was not getting any younger, with a much younger boyfriend, and his finances were not too healthy. Ossie took the children out every two weeks, but he wasn't sure if Nick enjoyed this, which played on his mind.

On the second of February, the awful news came about John Simon Richie, aka Sid Vicious, the Sex Pistol's bassist, who had died of an overdose in New York City at the age of 21.

Celia flew to America in March for a week, leaving the kids with her mother. The press hounded her for a story and offered £10,000. The pressure once again bore down on them both. In April, Ossie went on holiday to Tunisia with Peter Lee. It was a break from his worries. He sat around the pool and read books at the Hotel Miramar in the sunshine. They went to dinner and made the most of their time there.

When he returned from Tunisia, he went to see Celia, who opened the door and let him in and gave him a bunch of letters, which made him despondent, and a bill from the taxman for £6000. He went home to Nick and told him about his latest worries. Perhaps Nick saw another side to Ossie that wasn't so glamorous.

On top of it all Celia wanted school fees for the children. Ossie was worried about everything. It became difficult to get up in the mornings with the parties going on in the house. Marianne would bring back strangers to the home, and Ossie and Nick would be in a precarious position if she told them to leave.

Marianne and Ben, who were in the punk band The Vibrators, had a smack problem, and spent their time chasing dealers and smoking gear. It wasn't conducive to Ossie's creativity, but he had to put up with it. What else could he do? Nothing can be worse than when you live in somebody else's home, and you must be grateful, but he would have to leave for his sanity and peace of mind at some point. Marianne was four years younger than Ossie and could be a handful, going through her problems in the throes of heroin addiction.

Because of the lack of finances, Nick went out and found himself a job in a pub. He was a grafter and could soon turn the money over to keep his head above water.

In May, Ben and Marianne announced they would get married, and Ben told Ossie he and Nick would have to find somewhere else to stay. This threw Ossie into a tailspin. He became angry. He would have to find somewhere else to live.

Luck came his way when Chelita invited him to a Roxy Music gig a few days later. Afterwards, they returned to her house, and he told her about his problems. Chelita told him she was going to Trinidad in September, and they could use her basement flat, and when she came back, they could move upstairs for six months. Thank God for friends.

Ossie still took drugs, snorting coke with associates, relieving the situation. Unfortunately, everyone around him was on something, and he went along with it. One snort led to two snorts, and the never-ending line led to more drinks and late nights. He would go to work bleary-eyed. It became a hard life, but he loved the social life. Of course, he wasn't a monk; after all, surrounded by enticement, as Oscar Wilde proclaimed, I can resist everything but temptation.

On the 4th of May, Margaret Thatcher became Britain's first woman prime minister, with a landslide victory. The next day, she disassembled socialism in the UK, a sign of things in the future.

In June, Ossie and Nick went to celebrate Marianne's wedding. They arrived late. Nick was meant to be a witness, but the registrar told him he was too young to sign. Marianne laughed and said, "Never mind, you can sign at the next wedding."

By 1980, the commencement of a new decade, Britain had seen the rise of capitalism. The yuppies in Thatcher's Britain were out to make money and flaunt their wealth. The kids of the day wore blue jeans. Ossie loathed this. He really couldn't understand why they could be so unoriginal. The Hooray Henries and Sloane Rangers would soon replace the Kings Road's punks. Some made vast fortunes in this economic boom. Blonde-haired, blow-dried, dressed in their brogues and jackets from Balfour, bit by bit they took over. Then, as the freethinkers moved east for cheaper rents, the art scene disappeared in Chelsea. Many moved to the thriving Portobello Road in Notting Hill. Women around the country were clad in big shoulder pads. Everything was big; people chased money. Greed was the nature of this decade.

In January, Nick heard he'd secured an interview at long last for Byam Shaw; Ossie was made up for him. It was their first anniversary. They watched TV and Ossie made cocktails as they lounged around and wondered what lay ahead for 1980.

Ossie was still creative and swallowed pills to keep him on the move. He felt the pressure of not having his own home and relying on friends to put him up; it wasn't the best situation. A man needs a base to put his mind at ease. A good friend was the Japanese-born, American-raised model living in London, Marie Helvin. He loved her exquisiteness; she venerated his ability.

Ossie still had plenty of friends in high places. He wanted to stay occupied and produce garments; otherwise, the devil could strike with a vengeance. His mind wanted stimulation. Maybe he took drugs for the buzz they gave him.

In February, Celia said to the boys: "You are going to Greece with your father for the holidays." The boys had mentioned that they didn't want to go to LA. Ossie was over the moon. He booked the tickets for the following month.

On the 28th of March, they flew out to stay at the house of his friend Polly Hope. There was Albert and George, and Nick in tow; perhaps Ossie should have left Nick back in London so he could spend time with the kids alone in Lindos, on the Greek island of Rhodes.

With a number one album, *The Wall*, in America, Ossie's friend David Gilmour of Pink Floyd bought a house there and was on the island when they arrived. Dave, a good friend, invited them over; Ossie smoked hash on the roof while the kids played outside. The boys loved the sun, sea and sand holiday. It soon ended, and they flew back to England two weeks later.

MAK bought Ossie Clark Ltd from Peter Lee for £80,000 in April. The owners were Hans Hogben and his partner Noel Van den Berg. They were a couple of entrepreneurs who saw the chance to make money. They promised Ossie they would put on a show-stopping spectacle in New York.

Ossie had so many money problems that it created arguments between Nick and himself. Ossie and Nick had a strange relationship and to relieve the stress and break the cycle of constant worries they would go to Hampstead Heath for sex with strangers - a brief liaison with other gay men. They both craved illicit sex and went there for the thrill. It may seem strange, but this was the world they frequented; there was nothing weird about it in their eyes. It became routine and satisfied their need for excitement. No worries about women with their period pains. None of the problems of pregnancy. There were no questions asked as they made their way through the Heath, to find the spot, slip off the road, and pass into the undergrowth. Through the trees from Reddington Road on the far side of the Heath, where the luxury mansions are situated, traipsing through the shrubs you would come across the fuck tree, which lay horizontal on the ground in the middle of the clearing, a splodge of luminous paint daubed on the tree to let you know you were there. Condoms were strewn on the floor, and groups of men would cruise through the woods. A man would lean against the tree with his trousers around his ankles, and many men would come behind and take part, or they would watch in the distance. You could hear the grunts and groans, followed by the occasional yelp as one man playfully slapped another from behind. The pretty young boys would find a partner in double quick time. The older, uglier ones may have found it more difficult. They would have to take their satisfaction through glazed eyes.

Many voyeurs were too shy or intimidated and preferred to watch the action. No conversations are needed. It took a casual glance, or a raised eyebrow, to start the act. Some men loved the atmosphere down there, away from nosey judgements. It went on at night when there was no chance of kids being there. The police knew it went on but left them to it if they kept it between themselves. This was their culture. Men would cruise the area looking for a quick fix, no niceties, no cooked breakfast in the morning. Everybody knew why they were there. Years before there were gay clubs, this was how men met in secret and explored their sexuality. Either in the parks or toilet blocks scattered around the country, they would go there in a safe environment if you knew where to look. It was still illegal but tolerated. It was a different world from the straight world. I think Ossie became addicted to Hampstead Heath. It drew him back time after time; he couldn't help himself. It was free sex on tap.

Afterwards, males would leave, and new men would take their place. This went on all night and finished when the tubes ran in the morning. But first, you had to know how to make your way there. Some foliage would be splashed with paint to give you direction to a secluded spot. There was almost a mystical attraction to the area. Men found it addictive. No money changed hands. It was a free service provided by the gay community across London, who flocked there to savour the action throughout the summer nights. Of course, it might not be so pleasant in snow and rainfall over the wintertime. Still, many men would brave the cold weather in search of thrills. They trudged through the quagmire of mud in their wellington boots, looking for a partner who would be able and willing in the perishing weather. The things men would go through to satisfy their urges. The full moon was a popular time. When the rays of the moon shone, and the stars shimmered overhead, some found it hallucinogenic.

It wasn't a place for heterosexual couples. Instead, they would find their own part of the Heath for their fornicating. It's a twilight world many enjoy, a way to get your rocks off with strangers, no cheesy chat-up lines. They stripped all the formalities bare. Some found it so heady—illicit sex in the undergrowth, outside in the fresh air. You never knew what could happen if you scored some sex with somebody and came away sexually satisfied. It wasn't all seedy; it was another world, like couples dogging in car parks—each to their own. As we say in the north, there's nowt as queer as folk.

"You can have anything in life if you dress for it"
Edith Head

On the Dole

Ossie returned to NYC in December. His friend invited him to Barbados for Christmas and paid for his return ticket, but Ossie ended up on a bender and missed the flight to Barbados. He realised he had fucked up big time; could life get any worse?

1981 had been a lousy year. Ossie was still with Nick, but they had arguments, and his lack of finances did his head in. He still made dresses for one or two of his clients, like Angie Bowie and Shakira Caine. Some money changed hands, or he would be offered a weekend away at one of the country mansions; it was always good to get out of London and satisfy his wanderlust.

In 1982, Nick and Ossie found casual sexual partners outside their relationship. Ossie's finances were so bad that he always worried about where the money would come from. In addition, the situation forced him to deal with the DHSS. This affected his health and appearance and significantly strained his relationship with Nick.

Money is the tormentor of the planet. The meaningless crap we must do to get it. The world would be a much better place without it. Suppose you are creating art that gives people joy? In that case, there should be funding to enable you to survive without the constant threat of eviction and poverty hanging over your head. Some people are not cut from the same cloth as others and don't want to spend their lives chained to a job to earn money to pay the rent and survive.

Indeed, Ossie was a true artisan deep in his heart. He was lost without a good woman like Celia behind him. He came to realise this as the years dragged by. He knew he brought it all on himself. This made it no less tragic. Celia moved on with her life.

Maybe she'd had an idea about his gay side; still, they'd clicked on the friendship stakes. She gave him a chance to flourish and prosper, but it wasn't meant to be.

Both of them loved the boys, and what more could children want than two loving parents? Ossie was the wild and reckless one; Celia, the steady influence of the children.

Ossie became jealous of Nick. He found it problematic to cope with his younger lover, making Ossie possessive. He could be cruel and vindictive; they went through violent episodes. Nick loved Ossie, although he resented his negativity. Ossie felt his balls chopped off, emasculated and frustrated. Having no money can do this to a man. Still, he had to deal with it. Wealthy friends commissioned him to make dresses. He still had his talent and wit, so it wasn't all bad. At least he wasn't out on the street.

He didn't go out much because of his money situation. However, he sometimes went to the famous Colony Club, a private members' drinking den on Dean Street in Soho frequented by artists and writers like Lucien Freud and Francis Bacon. The owner, Muriel Belcher, was a coarse-mouthed lesbian of Jewish extraction. The people who knew her called it Muriel's Glib in the long-forgotten polari; she could speak the language of homosexuals and performers who wanted to talk in the not-so-open gay society of the early 20th century. She put men down with her verbal flippancy and made some feel like idiots. The males behind her would laugh and smirk when she didn't point it in their direction. She watched over the place as a belligerent warrior, sat on a high stool at the door. Muriel said she knew fuck all about art, but she knew about business. So she made the now legendary offer to Francis Bacon:" I will pay you £10 a week, and you can drink here for free if you bring me some fascinating people." Who could refuse this kind of offer? Soon it became the ideal hot spot in Soho. The performers and playwrights made it their home as they staggered up the stairs to the venue, which resembled a modest living room.

The mirrored walls made the venue look bigger than it was; everyone was rammed together. Nobody cared if you were gay if you had money and weren't a boring bastard. Muriel ran it with a firm knuckle; if you weren't a member, you could fuck off elsewhere. She worshipped money and took shit off nobody. George Melly, the ostentatious jazz singer who arrived in London from Liverpool in the 1940s, once said Muriel was a benevolent witch who drew in all of London's talent up those filthy stairs, like a skilled cook working with the ingredients of people and drink. Muriel's credo was "Drink up, pay up and fuck off."

Although she could be lovely, she would harangue the customers who had wads of cash to buy a drink for those who didn't—a character of the highest order, who knew everybody worth knowing in Soho. Muriel passed away in 1979. On her death, the club was handed over to her barman, Ian Board, and he ran it the same way as since its doors opened in 1948. You were greeted with "Hello Cunty. How are you today?" It was a term of endearment. Ossie would have loved this kind of humour.

Still, this wasn't the best time in Ossie's bohemian lifestyle. He would have been in a constant state of penury.

In February, he realised his desperate situation. He would need to sign on again; otherwise, he would be penniless. He went to the job centre in Hammersmith and filled the forms out. After that, he went back home, and Nick told him, "I will be at work tomorrow."

Ossie sensed more isolation. He thought Nick wanted to escape him and felt trapped. Ossie stayed honest with himself, and others did indeed have uncanny powers of intuitiveness. He could be a bastard and drive people away with his anger.

A week later, his green giro cheque landed on the mat, putting a smile on his face. He had £42.30. He rushed out, bought chicken and a bottle of wine, and scored some hash with his friend John. He bought a fiver's worth; it was top-quality Afghan hash. The texture and aroma said it all. He had a pleasant evening and slept well.

The money soon ran out, though, and a few days later, he was skint again. He worried about where the next bit of money would come from. He borrowed money from friends and family. He knew that he was pushing his luck, and people would give up on him if he didn't pull himself out of the shit.

With the enormous debts, which brought constant worries, it became difficult to get out of bed. Ossie let his beard grow and took a bath once a week, a sure-fire sign of his wretchedness. However, he still found time to cruise on the Heath. What a crazy world. He couldn't help himself and perhaps it relieved the stress. Who knows?

He became addicted to Valium, which helped him sleep at night and took away the pain he sensed in his chest.

In April, he rang around friends and spoke to Shakira, Michael Caine's wife, who said she loved the little black dress he had made her and would order some more. This pleased Ossie. He sent a few letters out to people, apologising for unpaid debts. At least he still had his morals.

Angie Bowie came around for a fitting, and Ossie promised he would have it done in the next week.

Towards the end of April, the sun beamed through his window. Ossie felt his mood change. He shaved his beard off and felt better. He finished the dress for Angie Bowie. She paid him £250 cash in hand. It wasn't worth declaring it to the DHSS. It could cause more trouble. Artists were often caught in this trap of working on the side for cash in hand and continuing to sign on. An artist should be able to create and not worry about financial burdens in the ideal world. What could he do? He did what he thought was best. And he lived a life of uncertainty, with a bit of work here and there, not perfect for anybody.

He got a little dog and called it Oscar. He loved the pooch. It was another mouth to feed, but he didn't care. It brought happiness to his life.

A blast of luck collided with his orbit. Somebody who would give him the fun he needed: Lady Henrietta Rous, or Henri to her friends. Ossie records in his diaries how they'd met at the society wedding of Cosmo Fry. Ossie loved the way Henri dressed, in her Edwardian cut. Ossie, by now, had turned 40; he was still a striking, mischievous sprite, bursting with charisma and charm, but he was down to earth and forthright at the same time. A mutual friend, the grey-haired RA Craigie Aitchison, introduced them. After a cursory conversation, Ossie straightway told Henri about his problems. "I'm going bankrupt and seeing a shrink": not the most incredible chat-up line, but it seemed to work.

Henri fell under Ossie's spell and invited him to the family home in Clovelly, North Devon. A few days later, he took the train to the country house.

He spent a few days there with Henri and her mother. Henri sympathised and couldn't understand how Ossie had got into such a risky situation when he had so many rich and famous friends.

Henri found Ossie a basement flat on Redcliffe Road when they returned to London. Ossie visited her apartment in Manchester

Square. Henri loved his visits and found him a creative, calming presence, humorous with an edge.

They came from different worlds. Henri wasn't used to dealing with the lower orders. Still, she made an exception for Ossie. He drew her into his sphere, and Henri pulled him into her realm. She found Ossie's honesty inspirational; he complained about the upper classes. They laughed and bounced off each other like friends do when they click, like two pool balls.

Henri became smitten. The pair spent the rest of the summer driving to parties across the city. She found him glamorous and captivating company.

They had a roller coaster few months. Ossie's mind still thought about Nick. Henri and Ossie had fiery arguments and split for six months after Ossie French-kissed a friend of hers. She gave them both a slap, and Ossie returned the favour with a harder whack.

He had a brief affair with her friend, but Henri couldn't stay upset forever, and they remained firm friends when they got over their altercation.

Around this time Aids began to appear on the scene in the UK. At first, it was thought to be some kind of cancer amongst the gay community in the US. David Hockney's friend Joe Mcdonald died of Aids in April 1983 in New York. This sent an almighty scare through the gay population. Nick was having more affairs, though, which made Ossie angry and jealous. He went to Hampstead Heath to seek his revenge. Were they both dicing with death, or did Ossie not care anymore? The stress bore down on his finances and emotions. He sensed he was losing control over Nick and his life. But he couldn't help himself; he was ashamed and excited at the same time.

Chelita returned to England and wanted her space. In February 1983, thieves kidnapped the racehorse Shergar. A ransom of £2 million was demanded but never paid. This was the least of Ossie's worries, with a horde of his own. They still lived at Chelita's but owed her over £2000. Chelita was strung out on heroin and tried to get the cure. The house was a pigsty, and she wanted them out. In anger, Ossie cut the wires to the electrics and left.

Ossie was forced to ring around friends to see if somebody could put them up. His nephew Jimmy Melia offered a room for them. Nick became moody while at Jimmy's and complained about everything. Ossie stayed grateful they had a roof over their heads. He remained passionate about Nick, who refused to have sex because of their living quarters. He became petulant. It would have been a crazy time for all three of them. Life seemed full of difficulties, but Ossie soldiered on.

Ossie's money problems caused angry outbursts between Nick and himself.

Under pressure, he was forced to rely on friends and family. A man needs a base to put his mind at ease.

Still, somehow Ossie managed to jet out to New York to meet buyers and arrange for a show. He became excited. But unfortunately, his luck didn't hold. The show never went ahead. Instead, Ossie was left fuming and he had constant rows with the new owners of the company. He came back demoralised a few weeks later. The owners gave Ossie a tough time; they threatened not to pay the rent. In a precarious situation, the pressure once again built. He sensed they were plotting behind his back; Kathleen, the machinist, told Ossie they were angry with him. But I'm sure Ossie gave as good as he got. There would have been explosive quarrels.

He spent time with Mick Jagger and his girlfriend, Jerry Hall, at their flat, but it would be a constant reminder of Jagger's riches. The more time Ossie spent with Mick, the more he realised he lived like a king. With the mystic at his fingertips, and magnetic charisma, he was wheeling and dealing with record companies, film producers, and the properties he bought. Jerry was practical, well organised and down to earth. Ossie could learn a lot from them. The situation of being famous, with money to splurge, then finding yourself with no money in a desperate situation, would be difficult for anybody to manage. His money worries must have been on Ossie's mind all the time. Yet he still went to parties, and his wealthy friends never thought about his position; when you have money, you think everybody has it.

In April, Ossie collected his bankruptcy petition from the Inland Revenue Solicitors; he owed taxes for the last 14 years. It amounted to £14,000, not an insignificant sum. Where could he find this kind of cash? Things weren't looking good. He prayed he could sort the mess out. Maybe he lived in a dream world. A saviour would come along. But unfortunately, this was when he began to fall out of love with the rag trade, and he couldn't get his enthusiasm up for the struggle ahead.

Celia was concerned. She told him his mother worried about his drug-taking; Ossie vowed to give them up. Celia and Ossie had known each other for 25 years; they had been divorced nine years now, but the children forever bonded them. Ossie appreciated her common sense and cherished her opinion. He would stop for a couple of weeks, he promised.

He procured the money to fly out and visit David Hockney in New York; he found David down over his friend Joe's memorial. Ossie spent a couple of weeks with David. Hockney said he would miss him.

Ossie flew back to London in May, full of trepidation at what lay ahead. The next day he had to go to the Strand in London for the bankruptcy hearing and fill out 30 pages of questions.

Ossie, by now, had moved out, and was living with his sister Kay, the jazz singer. Nick had found a new boyfriend, Robert. He said he was confused and loved both of them. Ossie had an almighty row with his sister Kay over Ossie's lifestyle. She didn't want him turning the house into a tip, and who could blame her? Yet again, it was not an ideal situation that he had to impose on family members and friends. But, of course, this couldn't have helped his mental state at all. Life is never easy, and things happen when you least expect them. However, Ossie wasn't an evil man; he was full of wonder for the world around him and he loved his family and friends.

Ossie's Swedish friend Ulla Thompson stopped him in the street, told Ossie about Buddhist meetings, and persuaded him to try it out. He went along half-heartedly but found he enjoyed it. Lotus Sutra Buddhism runs through chanting Nam myoho reng kyo. Ossie found it hypnotic. Many years later, Ossie would appreciate the teachings and embrace Buddhism. Faith is the essential requirement for entering the way of Buddha. This was the beginning of Ossie's journey with the Buddhist philosophy and it brought some light into his life.

Ossie was feeling lost and alone. Nick was running between Robert and Ossie, unsure of whom he wanted to be with. This made Ossie love him more and drove him mad. Nick persuaded Ossie to do some work with Radley once again, but this didn't work out. The collection didn't sell. Radley gave him two weeks 'notice on the 19th of October 1984.

This gave Ossie a major headache with the DHSS, who believed he had left of his own accord. He tried to explain that they had fired him. He wasn't given a choice. They told him they couldn't invest in him anymore. They found the complex shell designs impossible to make commercially. This disturbed Ossie's mind. He couldn't believe he was no longer wanted by Radley. This hurt his pride for sure. He remained no longer the leading man in the fashion world, and it was a sharp pill to swallow.

In 1984, London Fashion Week began its official entrance through The British Fashion Council. It goes on twice a year in February and September, puts London fashion in the spotlight, and has become an immense success with London buyers and media. Initially called Press Week, the first-ever fashion week was started in New York in 1943 during the war. Unfortunately, the Paris shows were cancelled because of the German occupation, making it impossible for US journalists to travel to France for inspiration. London's fashion week took a long time, but it is now on the calendar.

Ossie was still in contact with his friend Patrick Procter. He often went around to his flat to score hash and chat about their good times in the 60s. Ossie was studying Marcel Proust's life and reading many of his works. His philosophy was to be grateful for what we have in life. Desire makes everything blossom; possession makes everything wither and fade. I'm confident Ossie could relate to this rationale. Proust wanted us to not anguish at how our lives turn out but feel thankful for what we have. *In Search of Lost Time*, his most famous book, is known as the world's longest novel. He saw that to be happy and content with our lives, we must find a life which gives us a sense of meaning and purpose. Proust found his in writing, and I believe Ossie also felt the same in his writing. I can relate to this too. The world's drugs and money won't make you happy without a purpose. It took me many years to find my goal, but I hope you, the reader, have found yours. If you think about how many billions of years the planet has been here, and realise that if we are lucky, we may be here for perhaps 80 or 90 years, why wouldn't you want to find your passion and fulfilment rather than working in a dead-end job you hate? Choose to do something constructive and never stop learning. When people stop drinking, they lose many friends; but were they friends in the first place? March along to the beat of your own drum and don't be a people pleaser. Find your passion and stick with it; you will be much happier.

Ossie rummaged through the market. He spotted a pair of riding boots. This lifted his spirits. He still loved to dress with style even if his clothes were from thrift stores these days.

Celia flew to America to see David Hockney. Of course, this made Ossie angry and perhaps resentful. He was stuck in London, skint, while other people got on with their lives and seemed to do well. His head was in bits with it all.

In December, he came into money: he got a thousand pounds in cash for a dress he designed for Jenny Marriot, a nice little windfall. But, instead of saving the money, because of his need for change and escapism he booked a return ticket to Barbados. He wanted the change of scenery. He tried to escape his problems and forget about the bullshit in his life.

On Boxing Day, he headed to the airport and soared out to Barbados with a smile, full of joy at what lay ahead, to stay with his friend, the reggae singer Eddie Grant. He arrived in Barbados for a magnificent new moon. Life wasn't so bad after all. A few days later, he went to dinner with the singer Bryan Ferry, an old friend from London.

On New Year's Eve, he stayed with Eddie watching movies, with another friend from Warrington. The actor Tim Curry came over to join them.

"If you love something, wear it all the time. That's how you look extraordinary"
Vivienne Westwood

Barbados

It was an excellent buzz to start 1985. Ossie awoke on the steamy island of Barbados instead of in the dreary English winter. He was pushing the thoughts of his problems to the back of his mind. He made the most of what the island offered. He spent time lounging on the beach and savoured the ambience with the cool breeze and the coconut palms dotted around him. The landscape stimulated his sense of tranquillity. Although he smoked hash and took Mogadon to sleep, he was here to have fun and unwind.

A few days later, he received terrible news from Eddie on the beach. "Sorry to tell you this old boy, you'll have to move out." Eddie's wife had complained that Ossie had touched her up. Ossie was confused, remembering he had drunk a fair bit the previous night and danced with Eddie's wife. He never touched her up, but he wrapped his arms around her, and Bajan women didn't like to be touched.

Ossie made his apologies and said he would leave. Another friend on the island, Vicki Hodge, came to the rescue and told Ossie he could stay at hers.

Ossie slept on the end of her bed, and Vicki gave him the lowdown on her escapade with Prince Andrew. They both laughed. Ossie told Vicki about his clanger with Eddie's wife.

Vicki introduced Ossie to Kent Proverbs, the Bajan gay boy; Ossie loved his company and flirted with him throughout the holiday.

On the 19th of January, Ossie flew back to London, energised and invigorated.

In February, Ossie was back at the dole office.

Celia warned him to be careful about the Aids pandemic, widely reported by the media at the time as the 'gay plague'. Images flashed across the television screens daily—a picture of the Grim Reaper with photos of skeletal men were on the front cover of every newspaper. If you were a gay man, it seemed you were dicing with your life. The most famous star in the world, the actor Rock Hudson, was outed and shamed because he died from the dreaded disease. This also frightened the general population, who blamed the gay populace. It was a fear-provoking time, with the constant adverts about the virus screened throughout the country. It wasn't a suitable time to speak out about your homosexuality. You could get battered.

There was a real backlash against the gay community. They were blamed for it all. So many gay men sensed the shadow of death. The straight world thought you could catch it from drinking out of a glass a gay man had touched. The rumours were horrific and rampant throughout the city like a thunderstorm out of control.

The newspapers were full of stories of the latest Aids victims cremated at five times the average temperature. One report highlighted that a priest who frequented the gay clubs at night died because of his liaison. But it didn't seem to worry Ossie; perhaps he was in denial and just didn't want to stop his self-indulgent, hedonistic ways.

Ossie frequented Stringfellows Club at the Hippodrome. It thrilled Peter to meet him, and he pushed through his membership to the club in record time. The Hippodrome was the gold star club of the day. All the celebrities congregated there to catch the action, and were snapped by the paparazzi who lay in wait like vultures to get a sensational shot they could hawk to the world's news outlets or one of the daily sleaze rags.

Ossie undertook teaching jobs in Manchester and at the RCA. He was still in touch with Nick, who kept letting him down. They arranged to meet at Euston Station. Nick didn't show. This left Ossie despondent and angry with his antics.

Unable to understand why Nick was treating him like dirt, he resolved to play it cool; but would he be able to?

Ossie searched for a publisher for his diaries. Perhaps that could get him out of the shit. He couldn't hack it as an undischarged bankrupt. Bob Geldof was thinking about the crisis in Ethiopia, and Peter Stringfellow tried to get money out of Ossie to donate, which made him laugh under the circumstances. Ossie fobbed him off; what else could he do?

Ossie moved into a flat on Shrewsbury Mews, and life seemed to take a turn for the better, for a few months at least. He saw a psychiatrist, who gave him a chance to unburden himself and listened with a compassionate ear. Even after all these years, he was still angry over Celia's friendship with Hockney, particularly when David suggested Celia move to the States with the children. Ossie had a lot on his plate and he told the shrink everything, which helped his mind.

His friend, a former model, Agnes Kostrowski, reinvigorated him in May of '86, inspiring him to plan a lingerie collection under the name Rustle. Ossie loved the challenge; the deadline was September 16th. He was glad to be back at work. His shrink told Ossie to face his addiction to amphetamines, which had become a regular habit as the years went by.

Ossie found the drugs could put him in a manic state and help with his work; or did they? He seemed to thrive on pressure and deadlines. It was a mental thing and could be hard to stop. He was ignoring his bills at Shrewsbury Mews, though, and the Gas Board came along, went into his garage, and cut the supply off, taking the meter away.

Ossie stopped drinking for fifty days but relapsed in June and had a few pints; better luck next time. Finally, in August, his friend Prudence Glynn, the fashion editor of *The Times*, offered him a room at her home in Powis Terrace. Ossie handed over a deposit of £120 and moved in. Unfortunately, she had cats, and Ossie couldn't stand the smell. He had to tolerate it for a roof over his head.

Ossie was still making excursions to Hampstead Heath when he was in the mood for sex, picking up whoever was there and relieving himself in the muddied fields.

Ossie was glad to be back working and pondered why he had done nothing over the last few years. Meanwhile, the stench of the cats was driving him nuts. They were pissing and shitting all over the place. He still thought about Nick and his lover Robert but felt he didn't love him as much as before. He kept chopping and changing his mind. In the meantime, he had casual sex to quench his desires. Being caught up in the twilight world of drugs and sex, and his work, kept his mind off Nick.

He downed a can of special brew now in the mornings; it helped to keep his mind numb. He knew it was wrong but couldn't help himself, constantly combating his addictions.

On the 24th of September, his friend, mentor, and landlady, Prudence Glynn, passed away suddenly. It was a massive shock.

Ossie was distraught at her demise, and he also knew he was in a sticky position over the flat. A few days later, her relatives turned up to check the premises. Ossie gave them his deepest condolences; he sank into a depression over her demise.

He realised that he might have to move out soon. This put him in a panic. Where would he live? He was at the mercy of Prudence's family.

In November, his friend Henri saw Ossie interacting with his son and the world around him. They went to the National Gallery in Trafalgar Square, founded in 1824, and housing a vast collection of artwork dating from the mid-13th century to 1900. It was George's 14th birthday on the 26th of November. Henri sensed the love Ossie and George had for each other. There is nothing like the bond of father and son. Ossie would approach the framed masterpieces and he loved to inform and educate his son's young mind. It was a great and educational day out. They spent the rest of the day wandering around the polished floors, and speaking in hushed tones as they admired and examined each piece and moved around.

The months rolled by towards Christmas 1986. Ossie was asked to come to Warrington. He feared the worst, but was told his mother had left him £300 in her Will. He was thankful: he could do with the money.

He jumped on the coach to Warrington and spent time with the family, who were pleased to see him. Beryl had knitted him a jumper. He wasn't sure if he liked it. He stayed for one night, and on the 19th of December, he took the return coach back to London. He had a fun time with the family, making them laugh. At least he still had his black humour; thank God, he sometimes needed it.

Ossie spent Christmas day and Boxing Day with friends. Nick, George and Albert came over for dinner. Unfortunately, Nick was in a foul mood and refused to give Ossie a Christmas kiss. Ossie was back in love with Nick, who barely spoke to him all day. Ossie was happy, though, to have the boys around. He loved them with all his heart.

On New Year's Eve David Hockney didn't ring him; Nick didn't ring him. Ossie felt like nobody gave a toss about him. Nick rang him the next day but didn't declare his love; Ossie thought he was doubtless sat with his lover, Robert.

Ossie took a trip back to Warrington to see the family again in the first week of January 1987. Perhaps he needed their warmth and laughter to bring him out of his misery. Although he arrived with no money, he spent a happy week there. They took a trip to Chester. In the old Roman town 20 miles out of Warrington, Ossie thought how time had flown since he sang in the Chester Cathedral 31 years before. He spent time with Beryl, who always made him laugh with her sense of humour. She bounced off Ossie. As a result, he felt re-energised when the time came to leave.

Back in London, he saw his friend Wayne Sleep, who was doing eight shows a week at the Strand Theatre in a show called *Cabaret*. Ossie had an enjoyable time. They scored some coke from an Iranian coke dealer; Ossie knew Wayne needed something to keep him going with such a busy schedule. Then they went to Langan's Restaurant for an entire night, where they slipped in and out of the toilets, sniffing gear in the opulent surroundings.

On February 22nd, 1987, Ossie's friend, the pop icon Andy Warhol, died not long after gallbladder surgery at the age of 58. His death stunned the art world across the globe. They buried him at St John the Baptist Byzantine Catholic Cemetery in Bethal in Pittsburgh. It had been thought to be a routine operation, and the family were left devastated. They sued the hospital for negligence, which was later settled out of court for an undisclosed sum. He left behind 610 time capsules of his life. He charted every movement of his crazy lifespan at the pop factory. We have his wigs, cowboy boots, and Polaroids he took of his extraordinary friends. He taped phone calls from his friends and had them typed up; there is a whole treasury of his life in these time capsules, and I believe Blake Gopnik is now writing a 900-page biography about it all. Warhol was the man who defined 20th century art in America.

In March, Ossie gave an interview with *Elle* magazine. They asked him about 1967. Ossie said it was the last fabulous zenith of the individual. Now, he said, it's all people copying earlier big stars. Madonna emulates Marilyn Monroe, and Prince copies Little Richard. Nick Kamen is a clone of Elvis.

Ossie never held back with his astute and witty observations.

Ossie's name still meant something in the media when they wanted a story about fashion. Still, in the meantime, he was forced to shoplift for food, which was not something he enjoyed. He had a lack of cash.

In April, Ossie began receiving letters telling him to get out of the flat. This brought on more stress. It wasn't conducive to a happy life. So he ignored the letters and tried to continue as usual. However, after only six weeks of living with Prudence before she died, Ossie had no fundamental tenancy rights.

In May, his son Albert moved in to live with him. He was overjoyed to have his boy around. Then, in August, Ossie realised he had been living in the flat for a year. How much longer could he live there before being evicted and, heaven forbid, homeless?

Ossie worried about Aids; still, he went up to the Heath and enjoyed unprotected sex, I think out of frustration at his circumstances and for temporary relief from reality.

Ossie enjoyed the Notting Hill Carnival in August. However, Albert got sick from the food, and Celia wanted him to leave the house he shared with his father and return home.

In September, Albert applied to do a computer course at Hammersmith and West London College. He loved his father but moved back the next day with his mother. He knew his mum would look after him and fuss over him, like most boys who realise their mum takes care of them. The College accepted Albert. Ossie was happy for Albert to succeed, like all loving fathers. He wanted the best for his son.

Alas, Ossie heard the news he'd been dreading in September. He was forced to move out of the flat. This threw him on the mercy of Kensington and Chelsea Council to find him accommodation. Ossie set off toward the Town Hall a few days later.

He had to register with the council to see if they could find him suitable accommodation. He went to the ticket counter to claim his place in the queue. There were so many people in the borough who were desperate for a place to live. It could take years before he would be offered a place. So many are forced to live in temporary accommodation in hostels or hotels for years. If you are a single man, it's impossible to get a place.

It can be like winning the lottery to secure a home. Ossie waited there for hours. The waiting room was packed with claimants. Eventually he heard his name called over the tannoy: "Raymond Clark. Please make your way to desk 9." Ossie sprang out of the wooden chair. He made his way to the booth, unsure of what to expect and full of trepidation. He'd secured a letter from his doctor, and he had the eviction notice, which could help his case. The more paperwork you have to back up your story, the better. Otherwise, they will shoo you out of the door. Ossie had no money to put down as a deposit on a private flat and was in a crisis if this couldn't be sorted.

He sat himself down in the cubicle and explained his situation. The officer listened. He'd heard all these stories day in and day out for years. And they know how much power they have. People come to them when they have nobody to turn to and are a cigarette paper away from a park bench. Homelessness is rife throughout the borough, and many people are forced to live on the streets if they are turned away and told, "Sorry, we can't help you."

Ossie was flustered, but he knew he must use his charm, pour his heart out, and lay it on big time. He knew they could send him anywhere in London, outside the borough. God forbid they send me to Steeple Bumstead or some god-awful place, he thought. He kept this to himself as he hunched over the wooden desk and explained that he had lived in the area for years, and needed to be close to his children. He had been forced out on the streets through no fault of his own. The clerk listened to his story, and recognised that Ossie was connected to the area; he told Ossie he would do his best to see him stay in the borough.

He handed over a white form for Ossie to look over and fill in the questions. It took Ossie twenty minutes to fill out the form, which he handed back to the man, who said they might be able to help him.

Ossie scraped his chair back and thanked him. He left the building full of hope that this would get sorted. Otherwise, he couldn't bear to think about what could happen. Thousands of people were waiting to be housed. When Ossie hit the streets, he pulled out a cigarette and tried to calm himself down. He was feeling the pressure. A man needs a home to call his own; he was tired of being threatened by eviction over these years. It was time a bit of luck came his way. He couldn't take much more of this. It wasn't unknown for men in London to throw themselves under an oncoming tube train. The train passengers would just tut about the delay it caused.

If you have plenty of money, you are immune from these problems. Still, as Ossie knew, nobody wanted to hear about his issues. 80% of people weren't interested. The other 20% were glad you've got them. He had friends, but there were none he could turn to now. He crossed his fingers and hoped for the best.

A few weeks later, luck came Ossie's way. The council found him a flat in Holland Park on Penzance Place, a home of his own which nobody could take from him. He was ecstatic to be there, with his name on the rent book.

At last, he could walk through the cream-brick block of flats to his own front door. It could have been worse: they could have housed him outside the borough, and there are far worse places than Holland Park.

Ossie's friends helped him move in, and some donated furniture. He scoured Portobello Road looking for bric-à-brac. A considerable weight had now been taken from his shoulders. He bought a sewing machine, decorated the flat and made room for a workspace to get his life back in order. Finally, he could style the place to his taste and have friends over. Thank God he was no longer at the mercy of unscrupulous landlords. To rent a private flat in the area would have been way too expensive: he would never have been able to afford the exorbitant rents they charged. Everyone in the family was happy for him. He was in the right headspace.

He switched on the radio. Then, on November 18th, he heard the awful news that a horrific fire had started through a discarded lit match on the wooden escalators in Kings Cross; 31 lives were lost, and many more were injured. Although sad for the victims and their families, Ossie was relieved that his friends and family were nowhere near it. Life can be so cruel and fragile.

Ossie frequented the Colhearne pub on Brompton Road, a notorious gay leather watering hole in Earl's Court. It was full of men cruising for sex; and later found to have been the stalking ground of three serial killers who drank there over the years, Dennis Nilsen,

Michael Lupo and Colin Ireland. Men there wore coloured, coded handkerchiefs in their back pockets, showing their sexual preferences. Ten rainbow colours let the guys know what they were into. Alan Selby, the founder of MS Leather in San Francisco, claimed he came up with the idea in 1972 when their bandana supplier doubled their supply. To get rid of their stock, he came up with this brainwave.

It was a full-on gay bar. It wasn't a pub for a straight guy to go to. It would scare them to death.

Still, the music rocked, the atmosphere was electric, and Ossie would meet up there with Nick when the chance arose. They both loved the bar's vibe; it was a place to hang with guys on the same wavelength. Nobody gave a toss about who or what you were into.

Earl's Court was a 40-minute walk away from where Ossie lived on foot. He couldn't be bothered with public transport, which kept his weight down, so he trudged along the streets, through the High Street, Kensington, over Cromwell Road and onto Earl's Court Road, the epicentre of gay life.

He had his eccentricities. You couldn't pass him on the street without taking notice of him. He wore riding boots with long overcoats. He would stuff his pockets on his occasional shoplifting excursions with wine and cheese. A man had to survive.

People might be shocked at what he did, but he wasn't the only one. Notting Hill is crammed with con men and shoplifters, and every shop is fair game. You could sit outside the Warwick on Portobello Road and teams of crooks would offer you all kinds of things, from aftershaves to lumps of meat. Pickpockets work in the area, on the hustle on the boulevard of broken dreams of the Bella.

Ossie worried about his diaries being stolen and his debauched sex life being uncovered. However, he held nothing back in the journals. He wrote everything down with great insight into his world and mental state. I commend his bravery. He knew his revelations would hurt many friends when or if they were available; or maybe he never thought they would get into print.

He was now settled in the flat on Penzance Place. But, as Christmas approached, he evaluated his life and wondered what lay ahead. Money was low - he was used to this - but now he could get his life back on the upward trajectory. His mind was always on the go about how he could get back in the game.

> "Give a girl the right shoes, and she can conquer the world."
> Marilyn Monroe

Hampstead Heath

On New Year's Day, Ossie woke up with a colossal hangover; the skies were grey, and a stranger lay beside him in his bed. He soon slipped out of the door and left Ossie in his solitude, happy the visitor had vanished. It'd been a drunken mistake he regretted. He felt his mortality. Although 46, he felt he'd lived many lifetimes with all the difficulties he'd had. Perhaps the age difference between him and Nick made these thoughts enter his mind.

  Acid house music was new in London and Manchester, and the phenomenon spread around the country. The next massive thing in the underground musical revolution brought thousands of clubbers together. Ecstasy fuelled the dancers and it was perfect for gay clubs. Ossie heard the music played everywhere across the city.

  He sensed he was closer to publishing his diaries and was unsure how his friends would react to his revelations, which were scandalous in their honesty. Still, he felt it would help cleanse his past and was determined to go through it.

  He ran into Boy George in a club in the West End, and they chatted about George's problem with heroin. Ossie recommended he knock it in the head. It had been over ten years since he had met Nick; they still had an on-and-off relationship going nowhere, but Ossie couldn't help himself. The attraction strengthened when he knew Nick was no longer interested in him.

  Ossie, meanwhile, took regular trips up to the Heath. He met a homeless man named Martin at the end of January. Ossie brought him home, offering him some warmth and shelter for a while. Martin couldn't believe his luck and relished the idea. It showed Ossie's generosity and perhaps recklessness, but he couldn't change his nature.

  After about a week, Ossie realised he didn't want him there any more. He'd got enough of his own problems without taking on Martin's. He wanted to ask him to leave at once. Why did he do it in the first place? Loneliness? An act of kindness? He took Martin for breakfast and slipped him £20. Over the next few weeks, Martin stayed in various places; when cold and hungry, he rang Ossie, who relented and took him back for a night or two. He gave him clothes, let him bathe, and they had sex. Ossie knew it didn't make sense, but his generosity got the better of him. Martin said, "You are not like everybody else. You are kind and warm." Perhaps this pulled at Ossie's heartstrings.

Ossie took many walks in Holland Park with his dog Oscar. It gave them exercise and helped to clear his mind; he loved his dog, a loyal and faithful companion amongst all the trials of his life.

His finances were meagre; some mornings, he woke up penniless, and relied on the charity of friends and family. He really had been brought down to earth with a bang. This didn't help his depression, but he hoped for the best.

In April, they switched his electricity off. He asked his friend Tanya to loan him the money and she gave him £100. Another friend gave him another £100, which helped him pay the bill and get the electricity switched back on.

A few weeks later, his finances improved, and he took a trip to Madrid for a week or so. He returned refreshed.

He received terrible news on the 6th of May. He found out his best friend Mo McDermott had died. He took it with composure, though inside, he was shattered. Life again threw him a head fuck. He thought about his own life and wondered what he could do. Ossie and Mo had a lot in common. Both came from a working-class background. Their fathers had been at sea. He must have felt the loss in a big way; through Mo, he met Celia and Hockney, so it took a big part of his life away with the demise of his lifelong friend.

As we go through life, more people die. It can make you realise that we will all be the star of the show at our funerals one day. So, no matter how sad you feel about losing friends and family, you must bear this in mind and continue.

Ossie's son Albert was due to take a trip to America, and they discussed the best way to do it by bus and where to stay in New York.

Towards the end of May, Ossie saw his publisher, David Reynolds of Bloomsbury Publishing, at the luxurious Ritz hotel in Piccadilly. Ossie hadn't been drinking for a while but felt tempted when champagne was on offer, and he had a drink. However, there was no sign of the diary getting published soon.

He got a bit of work to design a dress for his friend Tanya, which gave him a boost and raised his spirits.

On the 9th of June, his 46th birthday, a day he felt glad to be alive, a friend from the 60s, Micha, invited him over to Marbella in Spain. This gave him something to look forward to once again. On the 26th of June, he got up early, stashed his pills and hash in the suitcase and popped around to Tanya's house to borrow money for the trip. He banged on the door. It roused her from her slumbers, and she dropped a £50 note out of her window, and shouted, "Enjoy the trip, darling."

Ossie spent a couple of weeks in Marbella with friends. His love of travel and the good life never left him. Somehow, he always got the money for overseas trips. Life wasn't so bad, and he had friends who admired his capabilities. He flew back to London on the 10th of July. He was picked up by his youngest son George and returned to the flat.

A lot was happening in 1988. Ossie was still chasing the publishing deal. He wanted an advance and felt £20,000 would help him out of his predicament. He talked again with Bloomsbury Publishing in July. Responding to Ossie's persistence, David wrote and offered him £10,000. He got it up to £17,000. Still, Ossie wasn't happy with this offer and wouldn't sign the deal. At least he knew they were interested, and I'm sure this would have comforted him in the back of his mind.

Towards the end of December, Ossie received terrible news from David at Bloomsbury Publishing. They couldn't sign a publishing deal because Ossie was an undischarged bankrupt. It must have made him shake his head in frustration; could things get any worse?

Phil Collins reached number one in the charts with 'Another Day in Paradise', which must have made Ossie laugh as he looked around his flat, where he was entering his third year. He had a sense of humour; along with his depressive moods, he still knew how to laugh. You had to keep a sense of absurdity in this life; otherwise, you would go nuts.

It is genuine and not imagined that talented artists have suffered through the centuries. Ossie was alive. There will always be hope where there is life.

He wasn't the only one living on benefits. There were over two million unemployed in the UK in 1988. However, he had influential friends. Often, he would be invited to parties. Though when he was skint, awaiting his £40 a week giro, he would go without food and cigarettes, which he hated. He could be on holiday somewhere exotic the next day, when friends invited him over to crash with them.

He often detested David Hockney, who invited Celia and the children to America. Hockney was loaded with cash, and Ossie must have felt like a down-and-out because he couldn't treat his family the same way. Still, I know Ossie could be flippant and perplexing with friends, but he was always truthful and would help wherever he could.

Well-read and articulate, he knew how to act around the wealthy and influential. He had made his mark in life. Still, he had spirit, and the past must have satisfied him. The glamour went to his head in the first days. He knew he was different. However, born an original, he would never die a copy. Ossie loved his walks. He took Oscar on strolls along Hyde Park and Kensington Gardens. Ossie would also stride to Hampstead Heath, which took over an hour and a half to get there. His love of the place disturbed his mind. He couldn't help himself; the lure of illicit sex was much stronger than his willpower.

Cruising along the toilets on the Heath had been going on for centuries. The men had their way of acknowledging each other; Ossie often went there when the mood struck; even if he felt ashamed, it was always there in the back of his mind if he had the urge. He knew where to go.

He used to go to the bath/sauna houses in various hotels across the city, where men would sit naked and look who was up for action. However, you had to pay an entrance fee to get in there. The bath owners knew this went on, but they turned a blind eye if it would increase their business. If you were gay, these were the places you would frequent to meet other men with similar tastes to your own. Or the closeted straight guys would nip in on their dinner hour and have a quick fix before they rushed back to their wives in suburbia.

We must look back through the last century and realise how many prominent artists of their day were gay and how their creativity shone through. What does it matter about their sexual proclivities? They created some of the most incredible fashions; Ossie was in brilliant company with Gianni Versace, Yves Saint Laurent, and Jean-Paul Gautier. Later the 90s fashion icon Alexander McQueen took his own life, and Leigh Bowery, the Australian designer, died of Aids in London. Creative people see the world differently. Many are drawn to fashion and art. Not all people who work in fashion and art are gay, but many innovators are.

In February, he was invited to a party for a friend's 43rd birthday in Morocco. He arrived back to find his telephone had been switched off. His benefits had been stopped because a letter he sent to inform them he would be away never arrived. What a ball-ache; he had to go through the entire process of a new claim with the DHSS. They can be like the Gestapo; still, he had no choice. He had to go through with it. Sometimes he felt that he would have no luck if he never had bad luck. He laughed bitterly.

On the 1st of May, he realised it would be one more year till he was discharged from his bankruptcy. Then he would be able to plan his life again.

Celia and the boys flew out to see David Hockney in Los Angeles. Ossie felt the loneliness of their parting; still, he was glad the boys would have a break.

Ossie was missing a car and rang David Hockney a few days later and asked him for the money to buy the vehicle; David said he would send the money in a couple of days. Ossie wondered if he would or if he was just being placated. Their lives were different, and perhaps Hockney was tired of being the middleman.

Ossie was a proud man in his younger days; circumstances changed and he would adapt. He lived by the motto if you don't ask, you don't get. If the roles were reversed, he would only be too happy to help a friend out, although it must have stuck in his throat going cap in hand to Hockney; still, needs must.

Ossie kept writing his diaries. He kept them up to date for when the journals would be published. He lived in hope.

On the 1st of June, the money arrived from the DHSS, and his claim was again back in the system. This gave him some breathing space, one less worry on his mind. However, I feel for his predicament; it must have been difficult. Life is full of difficulties. Now he lived in a council flat, relying on money from the state.

He was now approaching his 47th birthday. Life had changed; but his love for his sons, and his health, were intact.

His flat on Penzance Place was a short saunter from Portobello Road. Everybody knew him in the area. Life wasn't so bad. He never knew what could happen. He lived in the hope that his luck could change.

He missed his sons in Los Angeles with Celia and David Hockney. But he had to get on with his life and cope the best he could; sometimes, crippled with depression, he would somehow motivate himself for long walks to get through the day. At the end of July, he took one of his trips back to Warrington. He found out his sister, Beryl, was dying of cancer. This made him depressed. He felt his life was hard. However, he put on a brave face, visited Beryl twice, and tried to cheer her up.

What can you say to somebody in this condition? He held her and told her how much he loved her. Life can be so delicate. No matter how dreadful things got, Ossie appreciated being alive; perhaps her condition gave him some perspective on his own life.

Ossie returned to London and settled into his routine, existing on insignificant amounts of money and sometimes missing food. Albert, his eldest son, rang from Los Angeles, and said there had been an accident. David Hockney's favourite dog, Rupert, had escaped through a hole in the garden and been run over.

David Hockney was furious with the boys, and warned them not to end up like their father, and banned Albert from driving the car. The boys were angry. How dare he speak about their dad like that? Ossie thought Hockney was petty. Accidents happen. He wondered if Hockney would send them home, but he didn't. Ossie felt helpless in London. He couldn't do much, but he gave his love and advice and tried to console Albert.

David never sent Ossie the money he'd promised for the car. Maybe Ossie was already upset with Hockney. The problem is that when you are down, people will help you out for a while, but after a few years, it can be a problem if you have not sorted yourself out; there will be a point when people cut you off, and I think Hockney had reached this with Ossie.

In September, Ossie was invited over to Morocco. He was somehow able to get holidays even with no money, and good for him. He deserved a break from the grind in London.

In October, Ossie still owed the bank £15,000. He wanted £20,000 to straighten himself out. He felt like a hamster on a treadmill going nowhere. There'd not been too many moments of fun and laughter. Christmas and the new year came and went. We always think about life at the start of a new year, especially when a new decade is on the horizon. The 80s had been a time of greed and decadence under Thatcher and her government. Lucky for some, but unfortunately unlucky for many, and Ossie must have felt this more than most. He lived in one of the most exclusive boroughs in London, surrounded by untold wealth and desirable houses, without a pot to piss in. He couldn't have failed to see the irony of his situation.

On the 9th of November 1989, the fall of the Berlin Wall was announced as a crucial moment in history, marking the fall of the Iron Curtain and leading to the downfall of Communism in Eastern and Central Europe.

"Style is a simple way of saying complicated things."
Jean Cocteau

Tragedy

In 1990, Ossie relied more on Buddhism, which he'd taken to over the last few years. This seemed to help his troubles. He lived in the moment and took each day as it came. Nick, his ex-boyfriend, kept popping into Ossie's life, and they took long walks across London and through the parks. It pleased Ossie when he saw Nick.

The fashion designer Bella Freud, the artist Lucien Freud's daughter and Sigmund Freud's great-granddaughter, came to see Ossie after she finished her degree to learn about pattern cutting. She recalled that he said he could make anything, including bras and shoes, and he could. She learnt a lot from him and found him a stickler about getting things done in the approved manner, whether it was a t-shirt or a ballgown. Ossie taught her the intricacies of pattern cutting and to take pride in her work. After all, it is an art form and took years to learn; Ossie was superb and so generous with his time.

Ossie would sometimes go back to the RCA and give lectures to aspiring young designers. He enjoyed helping the students. They loved having him there. Ossie had fallen out of love with the rag trade, but he still loved to work at his own pace and design garments for friends.

Ossie tried to stop drinking and worried about his health, often checking his weight on the scales. Coming from his background in fashion, the last thing he wanted was to put weight on. He was many things; but his sense of style, like his mind, stayed as sharp as ever.

One of Ossie's good friends in London was style icon Duggie Fields. He would run into him on Portobello Road. Duggie, who lived in Earl's Court, was a brilliant artist, who'd shared a flat with Syd Barrett from Pink Floyd in 1968. They had exciting conversations; they had much in common. Both were gay and artistic and friends with Chelita Secunda.

One of his friends, Gill Goldsmith, requested that he make a ball gown, which gave Ossie a chance to make some money. So he set to work to get it done. First, he cleared the flat and created more space, which led to further work. Next, he made another dress for his friend Candina Lycett Green. A bit of cash in hand never goes amiss, and he sure needed the money.

Gill was pleased with the results, which did wonders for Ossie's sense of self-worth. He still had the knack. After all he'd been through, his talent remained.

At the end of March, a large gathering of over 200,000 protesters kicked off in Trafalgar Square to object to the poll tax introduced by Thatcher's government. Mounted police charged the crowd and there were over 300 arrests, which sparked similar protests around the country.

Ossie was once again asked to design a wedding dress for Cleo Goldsmith. This boosted his confidence. After all, this was what he was good at. So he set to work with transformed dynamism and finished it in time for the wedding on the 28th of April.

Months passed by. Ossie celebrated his son Albert's 21st birthday on the 22nd of October. Where had the time gone? He was so proud of both his boys. They were the joy of his life as he watched them grow into fine young men. The boys tried to stay close to Ossie throughout their lives.

In November, Ossie once again took a trip overseas, this time to the Greek island of Crete, for a week of fun and frolics under the Mediterranean sun. He returned to London in time to hear of the resignation of Margaret Thatcher; the working class of the country clapped and drank the pubs dry after she finished her term in government after 11 years.

He heard through his son George that David Hockney had had a heart attack; it shocked Ossie. Although not fatal, it made him worry about his health. His son George, by now 19, looked like Ossie did at the same age, he noticed. George was such a loving son, with Celia's caring nature.

Where were the years going? Ossie would celebrate his 49th birthday in June 1991. He'd stopped taking pills for over three months now. He was pleased with the achievement.

His elder sister, Beryl, was admitted to the hospital back in Warrington in January. The cancer was worse. Ossie prayed for her, but the news wasn't good. He wondered how much time Beryl had left, and on Saturday the 13th of April, his beloved sister Beryl died. Ossie sank further into his depression, devastated by the news.

His son Albert drove him to Warrington to attend the funeral the following week. His younger son George came along to pay his respects. Beryl was a big part of the family, and Ossie missed her deeply; it made him so sad that he started taking his pills again. When he returned to London, Ossie took another three months to feel better.

He went on holiday with his youngest son George at the end of his mourning, in June; they flew out to Greece on the island of Crete. Ossie took the pills prescribed by the doctor for his depression to give him some optimism. He felt his age and worried about becoming a burden to his children; he wasn't old, but that's how your mind works when the black dog hangs over you. "If this is living, roll on death" is a thought which passes through your mind when at the lowest point.

He loved to spend time with his son, who worried about Ossie and wondered why his dad took pills. Ossie explained that it helped raise his spirits and make him look forward to life again. He missed Beryl and realised how much he had made a mess of his life since the split from Celia. The boys wanted to be proud of him. George loved his dad and tried reassuring Ossie that things would improve. Their bond was strong and remained unbroken for the rest of their lives.

Ossie felt he was wasting his talent, but none of this bothered George: he just wanted his father to be happy. Times like this brought them closer. Ossie must have sensed the love, which gave him strength. They returned to London and reality towards the end of June.

Ossie felt better and was coming to terms with Beryl's death. He would have loved to return to Greece for three months and finish his book, if possible, but now, his finances were not up to it; however, it was a nice thought; he was so proud of his son and how he helped him through the rough time of his sister's passing.

Back in London, his friend Lady Henrietta Rous handed him a £50 note and asked him to make a blue suit for a wedding she'd been invited to. She also requested Ossie spend time at her house in

Clovelly in Devon to give him some time outside the city. He enjoyed his time with Henrietta and she did her best to help and cheer him up.

Ossie returned to London, determined to keep the flat clean, change the bedding weekly, and return to his old self.

He spent September in France and had a wonderful time; things had been up for him the last few months. He spent a couple of weeks at the invitation of his friend Mark Penney at a house in Dordogne.

Over the next few months, in London, he had constant back pains. He wondered what the problem was.

Nick told him he'd been diagnosed with Aids, but he should be okay with treatment, and it was nothing to worry about. Ossie hoped so. Nick meant the world to him.

By 1982 his money troubles came back vigorously. He was worried they would cut the electricity off. Still, he kept writing in his diaries. Perhaps the book would solve all his financial woes.

On top of this, Nick was in hospital. Ossie rang to ask him how he was feeling.

Nick said he felt weak, and broke down, sobbing on the phone. This made Ossie feel terrible; he offered to come and visit him. Nick refused. He wanted to be left alone with his misery now. It was a devastating time in both their lives, and Ossie was again back in his depression. He felt Nick's pain and would have loved to comfort him in this time of need. Ossie had a caring and generous spirit and stood by his friends.

Ossie was so shocked that he wondered how long Nick would have left on earth. He couldn't bear the thought of the death of his former lover.

As the months rolled by, Ossie kept himself busy. He met friends, went to the Tate and saw Hockney's seven paintings on show. He looked at the painting of himself and Celia. It was now 21 years since Hockney completed the painting. He must have thought about how his life had changed since then.

Over on the other side of London, a Croydon-born flat-chested Kate Moss signed to be the face of Calvin Klein in 1992. Alexander McQueen graduated from London's Central St. Martins School of Fashion as a young, gifted fashion designer.

As Ossie approached his 50th birthday, he met up with Nick. They walked the length of Portobello Road and took a trip to Hampstead. Oscar, Ossie's dog, ten years old, now became feeble. He loved the dog like he loved the family. A man in a pub remarked how the dog loved Ossie and stood there staring at him while he drank his pint. Ossie would cuddle Oscar and wonder how he would cope without his loyal friend. He loved his mutt and couldn't imagine life without him.

Nicks's health seemed to improve, which made Ossie feel good. On his 50th birthday on the 7th of June, his boy George rang to wish him happy birthday. Oscar wagged his tail and ran around.

He found out through his sister Kay that their elder sister Gladys had had a heart attack. Luckily, it wasn't fatal, but it was still another worry on his mind.

At the end of June, he and Nick went swimming in the pond in Hampstead, both happy in each other's company. It was great to see Nick in a good mood and able to have fun.

Ossie was asked over to Paris on the 1st of July for the Comme des Garcons, a Japanese fashion show founded in 1969 with offices in Japan and Paris, to be a model himself for a change. He flew out there ready to have fun and in a great mood. The actor John Hurt was also in the show to do some modelling. They had known each other since 1967. Ossie chose his shoes and wore a suit. He was paid 5000 francs. He strolled back to the hotel and bought some coloured pencils. Ossie enjoyed the glamour of Paris and the show, reminding him of his former glory.

Ossie kept writing in his journals and the next day returned to the show; they wanted the mature rebel look, which both he and John Hurt had in abundance. Ossie was still a good-looking guy, and with his imagination and dress sense, he could pull it off with no problem.

He returned to London on the 6th of July. On the 8th of July, it was Nick's 37th birthday, which he shared with David Hockney, now 55 years old. Time was flying by. Ossie had been living and working in London for 30 years.

He had back problems and always took pills for the pain. It got on his nerves, but what could he do?

At the end of July, he received the good news that his eldest son Albert had taken up a position at the Halcyon, a four-star hotel in Holland Park, as head chef.

His back was giving him so much pain that it freaked him out. His weight plummeted. He was down to nine stone five pounds. He wanted to do so much, but the pain in his backbone held him back. He saw an osteopath and paid to see him out of his dole money. After fixing his vertebra, he told Ossie he was in decent shape.

Ossie was under pressure. The doctor gave him sick notes that lasted only three months, which soon flew by, so he rang the doctor and asked for six months to provide him with some leeway if he needed to go away. It can be a nightmare if you are ill and constantly pressured to find a job. The doctor refused to give him a six-month sick note.

His back was so bad that he couldn't carry Oscar anymore. Even lifting his diaries, he could feel the pain. He questioned why he was still bothering to write in his journals. The pain drove him so crazy that sometimes he couldn't think straight.

Ossie was losing so much weight that he feared he might have Aids. He was admitted to the hospital in August. He spent a couple of weeks there. He was vomiting blood, but much to his relief, after tests, he found out it wasn't Aids. Thank God. He was discharged from St. Charles Hospital on Monday, 24th of August; it was a scary time, but he pulled through. He had significant problems with his ulcer, making him look rough and fatigued, but the love of his friends and family gave him the strength to face life.

In September, his adored dog Oscar died. Ossie was heartbroken at the loss. He so loved the pooch. Over the coming months, Oscar was on his mind. It shows me he was a good man. Anybody who loves animals has a caring nature.

Ossie felt lifeless, and spent much of his time in bed watching TV or reading books, and didn't have the energy to clean the flat. The black dog he suffered from was back. Depression can strike at any time. His sons rang and tried to cheer him up; it couldn't have been a simple time for Ossie.

He spent Christmas feeling sorry for himself, and couldn't be bothered eating. He was in constant pain, and was lethargic. Nothing seemed to cheer him up. He needed a holiday, but his finances wouldn't allow it. The barman in Ossie's local pub remarked how much the loss of Oscar seemed to affect Ossie and his personality.

We can only imagine his pain, but I'm sure if we all recorded our thoughts daily as Ossie did over the years, many sad days would be in our lives. I must admire him for this. And he had the added problem of suffering from depression. On January 20th, 1993, Bill Clinton's tenure began in America. John Major was the Prime Minister of England. I doubt any of this bothered Ossie. However, he had a rough year ahead. Nick had been forced to return from Egypt. In February, he went to Moorfields Eye Hospital in East London for treatment.

Ossie visited and found him lying on the bed with a drip to the vein in his neck and shingles in his right eye. Ossie tried to cheer him up and be a good friend; he felt terrible seeing Nick lying there. Although Ossie had his problems, he still had time for his mate.

He was still taking pills and depending on sick notes from his psychiatrist to keep him going through the bleak times he suffered between 1992 and 1993.

I contacted Mark, who runs a vintage fashion stall on Portobello Road. He called it Inner Sanctum. He said he was Ossie's number one fan. He recalled a customer coming to the booth. Mark selected pieces of Ossie's work and told the customer the history. The customer stood and listened and when he'd finished he said, "I know, I'm the designer." Mark couldn't believe Ossie Clark had come to his stall; they both had a good chat. Mark will always treasure this memory of meeting his hero.

On the 20th of March, Ossie woke up to the heartbreaking news of an IRA bomb detonated in Warrington. Two small boys died: Jonathan Ball was killed straightaway and Tim Parry died a couple of days later. The explosive device in a bin in the town centre injured 50 people, including a young mother who lost a leg and Bronwyn Vickers, who would later die from the injuries. The entire country was outraged, and in part, it led to the Good Friday agreement.

In the spring of 1993, the young British designer Alexander McQueen sprang onto the scene. Another working-class urchin is fresh out of art school. He held his first professional show at the Bluebird Garage in Chelsea, earning him the title L'Enfant Terrible, the hooligan of British fashion. Around the same time the Gibraltar-born British designer from working-class stock, the legendary John Galliano, made shock waves through the fashion world. Ossie must have noticed their stars were on the rise, and he must have been champing at the bit to get back in fashion; or maybe he wasn't. But, whatever he thought, it must have inspired and enthralled him.

Ossie knew what was going on in the world. He walked around with his eyes and ears open. Ossie had become a work of art in his apparel in later years. He could express himself; he may no longer be rich and famous, but he never lost his sense of the absurd and knew success could return. He was always looking for ways to get back into the industry, hoping that one day he would return with a vengeance. He wasn't some sad old man wandering around thinking about yesteryear. There would always be hope because he had many ideas in his mind. I am 100% certain of this.

You couldn't think he was lost and alone. He had friends, and I've heard he was always entertaining company when he was out going to friends 'houses for dinner and lively conversations; there was much more to Ossie than met the eye; sure, he had his memories and knew how to tell a fantastic tale, and most of all he still had his boys who he never stopped loving and would never turn his back on.

Then heartbreak hit. Nick Balaban died at the age of 35 on the 3rd of January 1994 at 11.30am. Ossie and Nick had been in a relationship for as long as he'd been with Celia. They'd remained close friends for over 16 years and had been through so much together. Ossie attended the funeral with Nick's best friend, Guy Burchill, who'd been at art school with Nick.

Nick was a beautiful young man in the prime of his life. With so much to offer, the desolation of Aids cruelly took him too soon. It hit home with Ossie; his much younger friend had gone forever.

In 1994 Ossie met a Polish lady, Jovanka Dejanovic, who'd lived in London since 1987 as an IT manager, at the Buddhist meetings, where they'd chant twice a day. She found Ossie to be bright and perky, and he always walked straight with his head held high, as if in the clouds. She recalled Ossie was tall because she would have to look up to talk with him; Jovanka is five foot eleven.

She recalled another time when she met Ossie at a party at Elizabeth's Mews in Knightsbridge. There stood at least 20 people on the roof terrace. Ossie spotted some fabric; Jovanka saw him take the material. He asked nobody and sat by himself in total silence with a tiny pair of scissors and nothing else. She could see the concentration on his face, and in 40 minutes, he'd made and cut a dress like a dream; she couldn't believe her eyes. It was incredible to see.

She recollected how Ossie stood up and said, "I love doing this." Jovanka said, "He told me he'd been a fashion designer many times. Still, I never really understood how good he was until I saw him that day. Fascinating to watch him at work. I honestly believed he would get back to the former fame he once enjoyed." Jovanka, although not creative, appreciated art and fashion and was knocked out by Ossie's talent.

Jovanka thought he was a particular person who could be complex and outspoken. He missed the old days when he would dress the likes of Britt Ekland and the many famous people he garbed during his heyday of the 60s and 70s. However, she still thought Ossie was on an upward trajectory, and he thought so too. He still clung to the hope that he would make a comeback. A letter appeared in the *Daily Mail*. The reader wanted to know what had happened to Ossie Clark. When he read this, he felt compelled to write in to the paper. "In 1983, I was made bankrupt. I fell out of love with the rag trade. During this time, I designed dresses for friends and had other interests. Like most people, I have had difficulties, but I had a great ten years."

"I don't design clothes. I design dreams."
Ralph Lauren

The Sicilian

1995 proved to be a momentous year in Ossie's life. He felt much better about life in the middle of January. He was out walking the dog he had taken in, Pippin, when he ran into a young guy from the island of Sicily on Holland Park Avenue, who stopped him in the street, and said, in broken English, "I am looking for the youth hostel found close by in the park. Where may this be?" The hostel is in the park, and many people in the area can never find it, so it's not unusual to be stopped and asked where it is.

Ossie took a few moments as he looked at the boy, the 27-year-old Italian Diego Cogolato, with his long black hair tied in a ponytail, and dreamy dark eyes, whose English wasn't that good.

They talked in the street for a few minutes. Ossie made a snap decision and suggested saving money: "Why not come and stay at mine, sweetie? I have a flat close by." Diego realised this was a godsend. His finances were low. The thought of a free house must have appealed. He agreed to go back home with Ossie. They returned to Ossie's flat, a five-minute walk away.

They talked and seemed to get along as they got closer to the flat. Both were happy to have found somebody to chat with. Diego was ready to get the rucksack off and take a shower.

Perhaps Ossie fancied the boy, 26 years his junior, or perhaps he was a good Samaritan and wanted to help him. Whichever it was, they both went along with it. Diego may have been a breath of fresh air in Ossie's eyes. Perhaps Ossie also felt sorry for him and wanted to help him, recalling when he first came to London. It can be challenging to survive in a city without friends and with nowhere to live.

When they stepped through the flat door, the Italian noticed how untidy the flat appeared, and over the next few days, he hoovered and cleaned the place. Diego was fussy and liked to live in clean surroundings. This must have pleased Ossie, who, like many artists, could be untidy at home because his thoughts were elsewhere. The last thing on artists' minds is chores. Ossie's shrine to Buddha in the flat comprised Sobbranie cigarette boxes with red roses he purloined from the nearby Holland Park. His inventive mind came up with the idea. Buddhism was still part of Ossie's life. Each day, he would chant Gongyho in the mornings and evenings. What Diego would make of this is anybody's guess. But, with a free roof over his head and a man who seemed happy he was there, he went along with it.

A sewing machine stood in the corner. The floors were lined with brown cutting paper. Goldfish swam in vases.

Ossie sewed and made clothes for friends. Nothing too extravagant, for small sums of money to keep him ticking over. He was under no pressure on the dole. He felt it would be problematic to take a job with the rent and council tax he would have to pay. And with his bouts of depression, it wasn't worth the hassle.

Over time, Ossie fell in love with Diego, who went along with it; perhaps he used Ossie for what he could get out of him. Friends of Ossie couldn't see what he saw in the boy. Orlando is an Italian guy who lives and works at the menswear shop Hornets, in Church Walk, off High Street Kensington. They sell classic British vintage menswear. In his younger days, he worked for Armani. He recalled how he would see Ossie a lot around the area. He said: "I could never understand what Ossie saw in Diego. His English was terrible. He was moody and surly. Ossie offered to do a painting of me, which he completed over the next few months. Although Ossie got my eye colour wrong, he did a fantastic job; I gave it back to him. He promised he would fix it. I never saw it again. This again goes to show Ossie's generous nature. He did this out of respect for his friend and didn't want money."

After the next few months, Ossie became concerned about Diego. He was depressive; Ossie suggested he go to a psychiatrist, who prescribed Prozac to keep his temper under control.

The problems were made much worse when Diego took Prozac for his illness and scored crack cocaine around the neighbourhood. The combination would prove deadly. Ladbroke Grove was in the middle of a crack pandemic; squats and crack houses sprang up all around Notting Hill and Ladbroke Grove. The dealers made big money, and once you'd tried crack, it was one of the most addictive drugs. It was hard to stop. Anybody who lived in the area in the 90s knew the horror stories. Shootouts and murders came out of the Stonebridge Estate in Harlesden, known as a crack city, a couple of miles away. They flooded the streets of Notting Hill and Ladbroke Grove with vast amounts of the drug.

Diego took whatever he could lay his hands on. He snorted amyl nitrate. He would swallow uppers and downers. Ossie tried to warn him of the dangers. Diego resented his intrusion and screamed "You are not my father!" This caused arguments between the two, and the neighbours recalled great ear-splitting screaming matches between them at all times of the day and night. They would be spotted around All Saints Road, where the Rastas hung out of doorways smoking joints, selling bits of rubber tyre to an unsuspecting punter for a fiver who thought he had scored exotic hash.

The All Saints Road was the front line of Notting Hill. It could be scary if you didn't know what you were doing and you could be fleeced in a moment. It was full of dealers, and the only way they knew how to survive was through drugs or music. The Jamaicans would laugh aloud when they saw the two batty men together hunting for cheap drugs. Ossie didn't give a toss what they thought if they got what they wanted. The problem was that Diego always liked it, and they didn't have the ready cash at their disposal.

Then they would go through periods of harmony and seem to get on. They would walk together through the park and Shepherd's Bush market. Often, both were skint.

Friends and family were concerned about Ossie and tried to warn him to be careful. But unfortunately, Ossie wouldn't listen. He was in love with the boy.

Diego, a heavy smoker, always complained when they had no money. He would search for fag ends to satisfy his craving. Diego also liked to drink. When drunk, he would cause arguments. We shall never know why Ossie didn't kick him out at this time. With his dark moods and bouts of depression, Diego couldn't have been the easiest person to live with, and he often would forget to take his medication.

Ossie tried to tell Diego he must get a job; Diego wanted nothing to do with working. He believed it was beneath him to do some crappy job for a few lousy pounds.

He took a job, got his first wage packet and told Ossie he'd been fired. They blew the wages of £120 on food, wine and hash, and it wasn't long before they were skint again.

In April, Ossie was discharged from his bankruptcy. He believed now could be an excellent time to renegotiate with Bloomsbury Publishing. The problem was that the relationship with Diego had become fiery and explosive. Ossie wouldn't back down with his sharp tongue and showed no fear. Diego must have felt frustrated when they argued with his limited English. Ossie's intelligence would overawe him. In retaliation, Diego drank and took drugs, got moodier, and acted like a spoilt child.

Ossie's sons felt alienated. They couldn't stand Diego, which must have put them off visiting Ossie at his flat. And who could blame them? They couldn't understand their father's infatuation with this ignorant Italian pig, who only seemed to want to get drunk and leech off their father; even though he had nothing, Ossie did his best by providing the boy with food and shelter and introducing him to his friends.

Diego got another job, washing up at a restaurant. He couldn't stick it for more than a few hours, threw his dishcloth down, walked out, and complained the work was not suitable for him, which incensed Ossie. It forced them to go to the Salvation Army on Portobello Road for a free hot meal that night.

When they returned to the flat, Diego played heavy metal music on full blast. He sank into one of his gloomy frames of mind and scowled like a madman. It would have been a horrible sight for Ossie, who had his own problems. It must have disturbed his mind to share a flat with Diego. Ossie likened Diego to one of Caravaggio's paintings of light and dark.

His friends shuddered when they saw them together. People were baffled about what was going on between this odd couple.

Diego's behaviours were gross. All he could think of was where the next drink or cigarette was coming from. So many of Ossie's friends barred him from coming around to their houses with this Italian lout in tow. Many Italians are hardworking and do an excellent job in the restaurants and clubs around Notting Hill, but

Diego wasn't one of them. He became a bloodsucker who only thought about his wants and needs.

Ossie flaunted his boyfriend around, proud of his good looks. He never noticed how Diego hauled him down to his level, and kept friends and family away. The problem was Ossie, a grown man in love, forgave Diego's indiscretions. They say love is blind, which proved true in Ossie's case.

Diego had been a heroin addict back in Italy and came to London to sort his life out. Who knows what drugs he took when he lived with Ossie? I suspect whatever he could get his hands on; I believe Ossie bonded over their difficulties with his drug problems. But unfortunately, so many drug addicts become co-dependent that it can prove difficult to break this bond as they both egg each other on. Diego didn't care about his behaviour. He wanted to have fun, get high, and get his hands on some cash to keep his drug habit in full bloom.

There were episodes of depression for them both; living in a small flat with no cash, they could get on top of each other.

Still, I believe Ossie never thought about it. He took drugs in one form or another for nearly 40 years for recreational purposes or his back pains. Although he wasn't a hardcore junky, he liked a spliff and a bit of coke and took heroin. Like many from his generation, it was the norm.

Ossie became closer to Diego and worried and fussed over him. Diego was a superb cook. There were happy times at home together, eating pasta and drinking wine; Diego kept the flat clean. However, their problems would worsen when they went out together. Ossie seemed to know everybody, but Diego felt left out because of his limited English. He became jealous of Ossie and would cause arguments to grab attention.

In March, Ossie was once again hospitalised with his ulcer. Although the pain was unbearable, after a few days it was controlled. Ossie was relieved to be discharged and headed home to the flat.

Diego was glad to see him back. The flat was polished. He told Ossie, "I was so worried about you. I drank three bottles of wine in your absence."

When cleaned out of money, they would march to Holland Park, go to the Kyoto Japanese Gardens, step in the water, and fish out the coins tourists flung in to make a wish. They did this when circumstances remained dire.

Ossie spent a week drawing a picture of Diego. He was pleased with the finished result.

His 53rd birthday came around on the 9th of June. He lingered in a good place. He loved Diego, and his sons were both doing well. What more could he want?

In July, his old Friend Mick Jagger invited them to a Rolling Stones gig at Wembley Stadium. They arrived early and went backstage, where the food and drink were laid out for the band and guests. The smell of marijuana drifted around the room. Ossie jostled his way past the groupies and hangers-on to get close to the bar. Mick hugged him; they embraced.

Diego begged him to get some cash out of Mick. "Your friend is wealthy. We need the money," he moaned to Ossie on the way there. Ossie wasn't sure, but he plucked up the courage and asked Mick for £15,000. Mick smiled and moved on to the next guest. Before he went on stage, the last thing he needed was to be tapped for money by his former clothes designer.

When the show began, thousands of fans crammed together and sang along to the songs as Mick strutted his stuff on stage. He howled into the microphone, shaking his hips as the girls screamed at the top of their voices, sat on their boyfriend's shoulders, craning their necks towards the stage in ecstasy.

Diego took no notice. Instead, he concentrated on getting wasted on the free alcohol, making a show of himself, and humiliating Ossie, who couldn't wait to get him out of there.

They boarded the tube at Wembley and headed back home, arguing. Diego was in a foul mood and sulked, cheesed off because they had no money. He couldn't understand why Mick Jagger, with all his millions, wouldn't give them a lousy fifteen grand. "Why are these people so tight-fisted?" he screamed at Ossie. "You seem to mean nothing to them these days. You tell me you were once rich and famous; now we have nothing?" When the tube pulled into Holland Park, they climbed the stairs, but it turned into a drunken argument when they got home. Diego rammed his fist through the glass pane of the front door. Glass shattered, and shards of glass flew. He screamed at the top of his voice, "I am so tired of not having money.

We have no cash; they have everything." He continued arguing throughout the night before he crashed into a drunken stupor. Ossie was furious and wondered why he was putting up with all this.

The council sent a workman around to fix the smashed window a few days later.

Ossie and Diego seemed to stumble from one disaster to the other as the months passed. For example, Ossie pulled in to fill the car up with petrol at the end of July. There was a lengthy line of vehicles; Ossie became impatient and shunted one. He believed the owner was taking forever to fill up and making them all wait, so he bumped the car with his bonnet. The owner approached him. She was an off-duty policewoman. An argument broke out, and a van-load of coppers turned up. Ossie and Diego were handcuffed, bundled in the back, and driven to Paddington Green police station, which deals with terrorists. They were dragged out of the van and up the steps. The duty sergeant put them in the cells to give them time to calm down.

Ossie paced up and down in his cell all night. He wondered what was going to happen. He couldn't believe he was in the shit again and thought Diego was a jinx. Trouble seemed to follow the pair around like an evil luck charm. But would his luck ever change for the better? He shook his head in frustration when he heard Diego screaming at the top of his voice that he was hungry and thirsty. The boy was a nuisance and a liability.

They were charged with common assault. A few hours later, they were brought to the desk sergeant and given back their property, told they were being released on bail and would have to go to court in a few weeks. Both smiled with relief. They headed out into the sunshine to taste freedom, tired and hungry but free. Calmed down, they realised they were in deep trouble. There was never a dull moment when these pair were around; perhaps Diego enjoyed the drama.

A couple of weeks later, on the 14th of August, they turned up at Marylebone Magistrates 'Court to face their charges. Their names were called and they stepped into the glossy polished dock. In his notebook, the court reporter scribbled away: the once-famous dress designer could be newsworthy for a few lines in the *London Evening Standard*.

The prosecutor stood and read out the charge. When he was finished, the magistrate told them to rise. Ossie was garbed in his suit, a buttoned waistcoat, a crisp white shirt, and a patterned tie. His grey hair was swept back over his forehead, and carrying a leather briefcase, he looked gaunt. Diego was dressed in jeans, a white t-shirt under a black jersey, a black bomber jacket zipped up, a pair of spectacles perched on his nose, and his long flowing locks tied back in a pigtail. Ossie was also charged with failing to produce a blood test and assaulting a policewoman. It was not looking good.

The magistrate reviewed their paperwork, weighed the facts, and gave them bail to return in September. The court reporter wrote the case results as the clerk shuffled the papers ready for the next defendant. The case kept getting adjourned until their decisive appearance in December 1995. Finally, they stood up in the dock with their hands behind their backs, praying the magistrate would be lenient. Their lawyer told them they could receive a term of imprisonment, something neither of them fancied.

When Ossie faced the magistrate, who looked across the courtroom at the pair, his words rang out: "Raymond Clark. I sentence you to prison for two months." Diego panicked when his name was read out. "Diego Cogolato, I sentence you to two months' imprisonment." Both Ossie and Diego's jaws dropped. They couldn't believe they would be in prison tonight; the thought horrified them. They immediately appealed the sentence. The magistrate listened to the solicitor, and they were re-released on bail. Both were happy to have evaded prison. They spent a woeful Christmas together, depressed, with not much money. Diego kept whining that he wanted wine and cigarettes; Ossie must have wanted to strangle him, and I wish he had done.

"I like my money where I can see it, hanging in my closet."
Carrie Bradshaw

Murder

One of the new friends Ossie had made over the last couple of years was a South African born graphic designer who worked for the BBC, the sharp-eyed Chris Paulsen. He became friends with Ossie from the Buddhist meetings. Chris, who'd lived around Notting Hill for the last 20 years, loved the area. Ossie's former celebrity didn't faze him. He recalled in 2022, from his home back in Cape Town, how he would go around his flat, chain his bike on the railings outside, and spend nights in conversation.

He mentioned how they would talk about many subjects. If Ossie needed to remember something, he would stand up and draw out the diary and look up a date to remember what he did on a particular day. He used these for reference and said all important people kept their private journals, and the world would know his thoughts one day. He wanted every word to be exact and honest.

Chris remembered how Ossie's illness affected his eating habits. He would cook everything fresh. He had some sharp knives in his home.

Chris enjoyed Ossie's conversations. He found him entertaining, although he mentioned Ossie could be abrasive and wouldn't suffer fools.

Chris, who wasn't gay, said Ossie never once made a pass at him. Instead, they stayed good friends who would sometimes meet up for a drink at The Cow on Westbourne Park Road or across the street at The Westbourne.

He mentioned how Ossie would talk about the industry and how much he'd learned from friends in the trade. He said his dresses were built on the same lines and put together to last, which proved true in hindsight. Ossie's dresses have been preserved for generations to come. Ossie said you could never underestimate the thrill a woman would receive when she bought a new dress which fitted well and made her look desirable. But, of course, they would blow a month's wages on such an item; Ossie understood this from an early age, so he did his utmost to ensure the dress would last.

His garments made dreams come true. Women gave him their requirements. Then Ossie would replicate them with his twist. Ossie hated the casual look, which would be discarded in a few months; he relished creating clothes for their permanence, the dexterity of tailoring a beautiful dress. Most people don't sew anymore. As a result, they miss the thrill of mending and cherishing their garments that could last for a lifetime with care. Ossie regarded himself as an artisan. It was a joy for Chris to hear him talk about his life and work.

Many of his former wealthy clients, he said, wore their clothes for years. They would rather pay for the best clothing money could buy, because they knew cheap was expensive overall, since they would be forced to keep buying new dresses every few months. Making custom-made clothing is demanding work. Ossie's prices stayed high. Another skill set was fitting a client out because of their different figures. Every one of his pieces had a personality. The cut, shape, and texture were constructed to fit the client's personality and enhance her beauty. Ossie could not abide cheap, off the peg dresses churned out in sweatshops across Asia - where was the style? "I may be a throwback to another time," he would say, "and people may say I'm old-fashioned, but they are wrong. My sense of style and fashion will never go out of elegance. People will come back and look at my creations when I'm dead and gone."

Nothing in the world is more satisfying, he said, than watching the joy on a client's face when he had created a unique dress. People will always appreciate excellence and artistry. Chris Paulsen would nod his head in agreement. There was a fire Ossie's his eyes, and passion, and Chris knew he was in the presence of a genuine artist. Ossie might have been short of cash and living in a council flat, but he spoke so much sense that it was hard not to admire his spirit.

He often spoke about his sons, proud of both of them. He thought his time would come again, and he could win back the respect of the public. Money didn't bother him. He became used to not having any, but sometimes Ossie felt hurt about the friends who had forsaken him. He didn't dwell on it; such is life, he would say, with a glass in his hand and a smile on his face. Ossie was still bohemian to the core and took life as it came.

In February, Ossie was invited to the RCA to lecture to the students. He still had much to give to the fashion world, and the students listened to him. With his vast knowledge of the industry, the undergraduates took notice. He told them about his early career and his aims.

The court appearance loomed, and they reappeared in March 1996 at 10am. Ossie wanted to plead not guilty, but the odds were stacked against them, with too many witnesses to the incident. The clerk called their names, and they made their way to the dock to stand in front of the magistrate. Diego fingered a Bible in his hand. Ossie looked defiant, waiting to hear their punishment.

The defending lawyer spoke after the prosecutor had finished. The magistrates then went out into the back room to decide their fate. Everybody sat down and waited thirty minutes. Finally, the clerk told the court to rise.

Both stood to hear their sentences. The entire court turned their eyes on the pair. The once-famous fashion designer and his Italian boyfriend were the most newsworthy case of the day. They held their breath as the magistrate passed sentence.

The magistrate said, "After careful deliberation, I have quashed your prison sentence. But, first, I sentence you, Raymond Clark, to a 12 month probation order, and you can count yourself lucky you are not going to prison today." Ossie smiled, stepped out of the dock, and walked to the back of the court. His footsteps rang out on the polished floor, breaking the silence. He sat back down on the wooden benches to hear the fate of his lover, happy to be a free man. Now all he needed to hear was Diego's fate. It had been a long couple of months for them both, with the threat of prison hanging over their heads.

The magistrate said Diego Cogolato, "I will also quash your prison sentence." Diego looked across at Ossie and smiled with relief. "But," the magistrate added, "I sentence you to 120 hours of community service." Diego stepped out of the dock and headed to Ossie. This astounded the reporter, who sat at a small desk scribbling away, expecting them to be sent to prison. He rushed out of the door and rang his editor at the *London Standard*; if lucky, they would get a few lines in the paper tonight and make the deadline.

Ossie and Diego left the court. Ossie said, "I told you, darling, we would get off" as they moved down the steps onto Marylebone High Street and made their way to the tube station, happy they hadn't gone to prison. When they arrived back in Holland Park, they went to The Castle pub and had a few drinks to celebrate their freedom.

As the weeks passed and life seemed to return to normal, or as normal as possible between the pair, Albert and George were sick to their stomachs with Diego. They didn't want to visit their father with the Italian around. They often complained to Ossie about getting rid of him.

Ossie didn't want to lose his boys and their respect. He also admitted that he was out of favour with his friends because of Diego and his anger issues and drug taking.

Ossie gave Diego an ultimatum to move out and find somewhere else to live. They could still be friends, but he needed to work and create.

Diego agreed to leave. They found him a hostel to move into in Bayswater. This proved to be great for Ossie's mental health. He could relax in his home and get on with his life without these violent episodes.

Diego thought about returning to Italy, but his mother refused to have him back if he was still taking drugs. So he hung around London and kept coming to see Ossie, who remained his one genuine friend.

Ossie's 54th birthday was on the 9th of June. His sister Gladys rang to wish him a happy birthday. Ossie seemed to have returned to normal. He was making clothes for friends, and his life was much better. He might not have had much money, but money isn't everything. Peace of mind and the respect of his family meant the world to him.

In August, Ossie arranged to design hats for an Italian friend. Neighbours who spotted him around the area at this time said he looked well and happy. They would see him walking around in the sunshine without a care, dressed well and with his head held high. It was good to see, remarked one of his neighbours.

It had been wise to get Diego to leave the flat.

Ossie attended a drink driving course the magistrates had ordered him to participate in. After, everything seemed to be fine. He kept busy and remained friends with Diego. They shared a bicycle to get around. Ossie kept it locked up at his place and Diego came around to use it when he wanted to. The hostel was a twenty-minute walk from Ossie's flat. Diego didn't have many friends, or if he did, they were people Ossie had introduced to him. He couldn't break the bond with Ossie, relied on him for friendship, and perhaps scrounged money when he knew Ossie had received his dole. Ossie didn't seem to mind him coming around now. They were not living together full time. The neighbours were relieved: they didn't have to listen to their slanging matches and violent episodes.

It had been 18 months since Ossie and Diego had become friends and lovers. Ossie was still going to Holland Park to walk and do his Gongyo; he recorded his thoughts in the diaries. He had been a practising Buddhist for many years, which seemed to give him inner calm and help him clear his mind.

On August 5th, Ossie left a message for Diego telling him he would be in Holland Park and to come along if he wanted to. He still worried about Diego and his constant depression. This shows how caring Ossie was.

On the morning of the 6th of August 1996, neighbours saw Ossie walk through the small block of flats' courtyard. He seemed fine. There appeared to be nothing to worry about. However, around 8pm, his neighbour spotted Diego on the bike. About an hour later, Diego left.

Nobody would ever have thought that what happened in the flat would make global news. Yet, the following morning, in the early hours, Diego searched for a red phone box, telephoned the police in Richmond and said "I think I may have killed somebody." Diego headed to Richmond Park and the police arrived to find the gates locked. They scaled the walls and found him howling at the moon. Diego was arrested and taken into custody.

In the meantime, the policeman sent to Ossie's flat arrived on the scene, and was shocked and horrified at what he saw. He couldn't believe somebody could be so brutal. There was blood all over the place, splattered on the walls. Ossie was slumped on his bed. Ossie must have fought to save his life. It brings tears to my eyes when I think about it now. This man, throughout his life, tried to do his best. But unfortunately, he was snuffed out by a madman high on drugs.

The policeman immediately phoned for backup, and the ambulance arrived at Ossie's flat not long after. They cordoned the area off, and the forensic team went to work. Ossie's remains were placed into a body bag a few hours later. He was carried down the stairs and loaded into the back of the ambulance. The press snapped photos as the body was driven to the mortuary.

Later in the evening of the 7th of August, Celia and the boys' hearts sank. They were distraught when they learnt about the tragedy.

The following morning, on the 8th of August, the news of the brutal murder broke worldwide. They made much about Ossie and Celia's 60s heyday in the press, but Celia didn't want to speak with the media; and who could blame her? She was concerned about her sons and wanted the family to be left alone to grieve in peace.

A few weeks later, the funeral was arranged at the nearby Kensal Green Cemetery on Harrow Road in North Kensington. The cortege drove through the black-iron gates to the church. After the ceremony, friends and family gathered around the graveside as his coffin was lowered. A man who brought so much to the world was now at peace, in his ultimate resting place. A headstone was erected with the inscription 'Raymond Ossie Clark 9-6-42/ 6-8-96 with love from his sons Albert and George'. The boys were overwhelmed by the loss of their father and would never fully recover from the tragedy.

His sons have a park bench dedicated to Ossie behind the Japanese Kyoto Gardens in Holland Park. As a result, people can sit and reflect on their life. Ossie loved the park. It was his escape from the world, when he would walk for miles. His little sanctuary was a beautiful retreat from the city and all its pressures. I recommend going there if you live or work in West London or come to London for a visit and want to feel close to Ossie.

"Fashion is about dreaming and making other people dream."
Donatella Versace

Aftermath

28-year-old Diego Cogolato was brought before the magistrates in Marylebone in a baggy white forensics suit. He didn't know whether he was losing his mind and began to realise what he had done, flanked by two policemen and in an anxious state. The prosecutor told the magistrates he'd been charged with the murder of Raymond Clark on the 6th of August at his home at 17b Penzance Place. As the case progressed, the magistrate listened. Finally, the prosecution asked for him to be remanded in custody while they inquired further.

Diego held his head in shame when asked whether he was guilty. He mumbled, "Not guilty." In a state, he knew he was in deep shit. How could he have done this? He had murdered his best friend, the man who loved him, gave him a roof over his head, and cared for him. Now he was being condemned as a monster; he must have realised with growing dread that he wouldn't see freedom for many years.

His lawyer told him there was only one sentence if he was found guilty of murder; it would be a mandatory life sentence. There could be no other outcome. Diego remained petrified. How could he cope with the guilt and being locked up in this filthy English prison?

His stomach and mind were in turmoil. He wanted to run away and return to Italy, but this would be impossible. This was his second time in court, and there would be no community service this time.

The reality of what he had done would have hit him like a brick in the face. Terrified about spending the rest of his days in prison, did he feel remorseful? Did he realise what he'd done? Was he still in a psychotic state? The drugs would have to be administered in the prison hospital. He would have to have psychiatric reports made on his mental health.

He returned to custody. The policeman took Diego by the arm and led him down the steps where he was fed and awaited a police car. The press was all over the case. Diego was taken from his cell, the handcuffs locked tight on his wrists. He was taken out of the back doors of the courtroom, loaded into a Black Maria and driven to Wormwood Scrubs with two police officers. The prison gates clanged open when they arrived and he was driven to the reception. They unlocked the back doors of the vehicle. He stepped out into the courtyard. He was brought before the reception officer and processed. His belongings were sealed in a brown envelope to be locked away until he was released. He was told to undress, and was stripped and searched. They checked that he was carrying no contraband and requested he bend over. An officer looked up his arse cheeks to see nothing was secreted there. His photo was taken, and his fingerprints were recorded.

He was issued his prison number written on a cell card, which would be his official number for the rest of his sentence. Everything was recorded: his age, date of birth, where he came from, and what requirements he had to see a doctor or a shrink. The other prisoners knew he was there for murder, so they were wary of him.

When this was over, he was given a towel and told to shower. When he returned, he was issued with his bedding and led into the hospital wing, the noise reverberating in his ears of hundreds of prisoners shouting across each other. He was frightened out of his wits at what lay ahead of him. Finally, he was brought to the landing with his prison issue bedding under his arm.

A prison officer walked in front of him with the keys jangling. Their footsteps rang out on the metal landing. The prison officer stopped in front of a cell door, unlocked it, and pushed it open. He pointed into the cell and said "Get in there." Diego was petrified. He walked into the cell and laid his bedding down on a bunk bed.

Diego heard the cell door bang shut and the bolt being drawn back. He looked around the enclosure, at the the iron bars, and the realisation of what he had done circled around him. He lay on his bunk and wrapped his arms around himself in a state of confusion. His brain was delirious, wondering what he had done and why he had done this.

The new surroundings were a shock to his system. The first day in prison is like a nightmare for any new inmate if you have never been through the gates.

Many prisoners are bullied, and some commit suicide under the circumstances. They cannot manage being locked up. No matter what people think, they are not holiday camps. Although Diego deserved to be there, taking your freedom away is no joke. Many prisoners are there for petty offences, growing weed or a bit of shoplifting.

The next day he was unlocked for breakfast, and soon he was brought before the prison doctor, who checked his mental health. He'd been prescribed medication. Many shrinks saw him over the following weeks and months. Upon his arrest, doctors found traces of Prozac along with the amphetamines he had taken. In their view, he was suffering from a mental illness; this could be helpful in his case later. His lawyer visited him and they prepared the case for his defence in the prison visiting room, filled with tables where friends and family came to see their relatives. There was a small canteen where you could buy coffee and sandwiches on the visits.

Diego was still an unconvicted prisoner until he was sentenced. He could have visits, and was allowed to have food and magazines sent to him. Life was far from being comfortable, yet he was still alive. Ossie was not. Diego deserved everything coming his way. The prison chaplain came to him in his cell, and they talked for a while. He handed him a Bible so he could look for solace. Over the next few months, he was brought before the courts while the prosecution and defence prepared their cases.

The magistrate remanded Diego into custody, to be sent to the Old Bailey to face his punishment. The magistrates can only sentence you to 12 months in prison, so his case had to go to the Crown Court. The prisoners heard the news on their radios. Diego made headlines in the national press. It was only a matter of time before he would be handed a life sentence. Everyone knew this would be his retribution.

It took seven months before his appearance at the Old Bailey to face justice on the 17th of March 1997. From his prison cell, where he spent a restless night, he knew today was the day. They unlocked him in the morning, took him through the wing where he ate his breakfast and transported him through the prison with other prisoners to be sentenced. Handcuffed, he was brought to the prison van. He stepped into the vehicle.

The engine rumbled to life as they drove up to the gates, which were buzzed open. The sweatbox headed out into the streets. Diego glimpsed people walking and going about their business. He wished he was free to do as he pleased. They flashed by the shops and pubs on their way to the court. It took over an hour to get to the Old Bailey. Reporters outside with photographers with long lens cameras took photos, hoping to get a shot of him to make the evening papers.

He knew the drill. He was led into the court with a blanket over his head. The case had drawn huge media interest. Once inside the court building, the handcuffs were removed, and he was again placed in a cell. He waited there, worried sick, until the door was unlocked, and his barrister Margaret Barnes arrived, briefcase in hand.

They sat together and discussed what would happen. The barrister said he could plead guilty with diminished responsibility. She had spoken with the prosecution, and after reading the reports on his case, they had decided to let him go for this. Diego was unsure what this would mean, but he was more than ready to agree to anything if it meant less time in prison. He missed the family in Italy. He found the incarceration hard to bear. After the barrister left, the cell door banged shut. Diego was left to wait for his case to be called. He felt sick with worry. It was hard to concentrate. He was thousands of miles from home, and sensed it would be a long time before he tasted freedom again.

He smoked like a man who was about to be sentenced to death. He kept asking for a light and couldn't keep his mind focused. He was scared; no matter what the barrister had told him, he knew nothing would matter until he was sentenced.

When the cell door opened later in the morning, he had to prepare himself to face the court. Footsteps echoed on the steps. He was brought up from the cells below to meet the judge in his red gown and wig. Nervous as hell, Diego knew he might go to prison for the rest of his life. The court was packed with reporters and a curious public to see justice meted out. It was a long day as the charges were read out, and the prosecutor outlined the case. Diego felt the pressure and was praying the judge would show some leniency. He'd been in prison for the last seven months, drug-free and back on the medication which kept him in check.

The name of Ossie Clark was enough to draw colossal interest in the case. Diego was sure things would not be good if he had to spend the rest of his life behind bars.

He must have been regretting his actions. Who knows what went through his mind on the night of the murder? Did he have a conscience over the terrible crime? It wasn't easy to tell. His mother would have worried about his mental health and how he would cope, but nobody else cared. They wanted the judge to throw the key away and let him rot in jail, especially Ossie's family. Many people were in a rage about the atrocity he had committed.

The court was told that Diego arrived at Ossie's flat high on Prozac and amphetamines. There was a massive argument between the two, but what they said was never revealed. What caused the fight? In a psychotic rage, Diego thought he was the messiah and Ossie the devil. So he brandished a kitchen knife, struck Ossie 37 times, smashed a terracotta pot over his head, and left him dead on the floor before escaping shoeless out of the door. The reason he gave for such violence was that he thought Ossie would be reincarnated and come back for his revenge.

Diego pleaded guilty to manslaughter with diminished responsibility. If a doctor had not prescribed Prozac, the defence wouldn't have had a case for manslaughter. It would have been a murder case, as the courts hold a defendant responsible for actions taken when under the influence of alcohol or drugs, because the mental state is self-induced.

The judge, Mr Justice Douglas Brown, left the room to consider his sentence; Diego sat back down. His stomach was in knots as he gazed around the courtroom. His mind was in pieces, thinking about how this would end. There was a buzz in the court as the reporters and people in the gallery talked amongst themselves about the sentence he must receive. It wasn't too long before the judge decided. When the judge returned, the court was told to rise. Everybody sat back down apart from Diego, who stood in the dock holding the brass rail to support him.

The judge said, "You killed your friend in a frenzied attack while in a psychotic state, which prescribed and illicit drugs may have bought on. Therefore, I have accepted your plea for diminished responsibility. I will sentence you to six years' imprisonment."

Diego felt a weight come off his shoulders. His mind counted how long before he might be back out on the street: with the time spent on remand, which would come off the sentence, he might be out in three years or fewer if he received parole. How could this be possible? His prayers had been answered. It seemed almost too lenient. How could a man commit an atrocious murder and receive a paltry sentence?

It seemed a mockery of Ossie's life. But once a sentence is passed, nobody can do anything. The prison officer tapped Diego on the shoulder. He was led down the stairs and placed back in the cell until later in the day, when he was driven back to the Scrubs, where he would spend a few months before being allocated to another prison.

Ossie's friends and family were dumbstruck when Diego was sentenced to six years. This wasn't true. How could the judge be so lenient that it sent shock waves worldwide?

His family in Warrington couldn't get their heads around it. How did his beloved sons feel? We can only imagine it must have been a terrible time for them all; it must have felt an unfair injustice had been dished out to the monster that killed their father. Not one person could understand why this had happened. Diego walked down the stone steps of the Old Bailey, his heart beating against his chest, mouth dry, shocked, as he'd prepared himself for a life sentence. He must have felt so relieved as he lay in his prison bunk that night in Wormwood Scrubs.

Over the years, friends of Ossie went to see Diego. He told them he had arrived at Ossie's flat to find him in bed, in no mood to see him. Diego lit a joss stick; Ossie said something, and he flew into a murderous rage. Diego said his temper conducted this heinous crime; he said that in his mind, at the time, he thought Ossie was the devil incarnate. However, Diego admitted he still loved Ossie and couldn't believe he had killed his lover in such a cruel manner; it was something he would have to live with for the rest of his life.

Diego slipped out of the prison gates without fanfare when he was released. He must have felt like one of the luckiest men alive.

I have searched the Internet to find out where he went after his release. He seems not to have left a digital trace and perhaps changed his online name. Still, after spending time back in Scilly, he is believed to have gone to live in Dublin under a different name. Sicilians are known for saying nothing, and we can assume there are reporters out there searching for his version of the tragic event. Maybe one day, he will come forward with his reasons. I believe he was dazed and confused, and perhaps the judge thought it was a lovers' tiff which went wrong between two homosexuals and didn't take the case seriously.

"I want people to see the dress but focus on the woman"
Vera Wang

Epilogue

Of all the newspaper articles that appeared after Ossie's death, I think the most moving was by Ossie's friend, Guy Burch, in the *Gay Times*. I have spoken to Guy Burch, and asked his permission to use it. He knew Ossie in the 80s and I think he summed Ossie up later in life. We should celebrate his achievements and realise he was a man with all the problems we all encounter.

"When news of the murder of the dress designer Ossie Clark was announced, the following stories focused on his heyday and subsequent 'sad decline'. Obituaries pictured a man slowly spiralling downwards after bankruptcy and a broken marriage. But this is not the complete story to friends like me who never knew him as the darling of the sixties and seventies.

"It was predictable that any relationship outside Ossie's marriage to the fabric designer, Celia Birtwell, would be given a sordid spin in the press. And that there would be no mention of the man who, until he died in 1994, was the most critical person in Ossie's life after his sons, Albert and George.

"Ossie first met Nick Balaban at the Sombrero club in Kensington. For most of the eighties, they lived together in a house loaned to them by Chelita Secunda, the wife of Mack Bolan's manager, Tony Secunda. Ossie had helped get her off heroin, locking her in her room to do cold turkey. She had moved to the Caribbean to keep away from the drug lifestyle. Ossie filled her house with the remnants of his past affluence, supplemented by new treasures, often slightly dishevelled or moth-eaten, from hunting expeditions on the Portobello Road. Oriental carpets, Lalique glass, Hockney prints (he hid a few stained and unsigned pulls from his creditors in their frames below drawings by his children) and *Vogue* photographs fought for space with piles of clothes, dress patterns and two King Charles spaniels appropriately named Oscar and Bosie. Reports of Ossie's death made a great play that he lived in a later squalid flat that was 'artistically neglected'. This was Ossie's typical standard of housekeeping. Wonderfully gifted but utterly impractical, for Ossie, orderliness mattered little, but style mattered a lot. If it was a choice between eating or having his shirts laundered, he (and Nick) went hungry. My partner Richard was in America on a six-month sabbatical when Nick left him. We regularly met to 'do 'the market. Afterwards, he would cook dinner for me in return for a bit of tidying, picking pins out of the rugs and hoovering.

"Though Ossie was depressed by his divorce and bankruptcy, he and Nick lived happily together for about as long as he and Celia had done before. Money and space were in short supply, but his imagination remained as fertile as ever. Unfortunately, commercial dressmaking had lost much of its appeal. Still, he made incredible, uniquely inventive one-off commissions for a few loyal friends who paid by barter: a ticket to America or his monthly bills. Not long before his death, he had made an Indian wedding dress.

"Writing became essential to him, too, as he chronicled his life in extraordinary Pepysian diaries beautifully written in different colours and often decorated with delicate drawings. The people captured in them were sometimes asked to add their comments: Marc Bolan had added a poem about death not long before his own.

"In the last few years, Ossie had talked about publishing these diaries. But he never got around to it partly because he was a perfectionist and somewhat because he loathed 'kiss-and-tell' celebrities. He had often been asked to tell the intimate sex-and-drugs secrets of those many friends who remained famous long after Ossie's renown faded, but he always steadfastly refused. He was loyal even to those who, it seemed to me, showed him little generosity once he could no longer shower them with dresses or champagne. The glitter that Chelita put on Bolan's eyes and launched Glam Rock and the whole 1970s glam disguised a cruel commercial world, not given to generosity or artistic support. I saw little help come his way from others; some who had been artistic heroes of mine seemed almost callously unmoved. Many of the women he introduced me to from that time were tough and rhino-skinned, having survived being thrown aside or commercial falls themselves frequently. I liked many of them for it: I've always despised women who are cutesy or doting on men, preferring Barbara Hepworths to Marilyn Monroes.

"Women like Pauline Fordham had been addicted to heroin for a decade. And would keep disappearing to chase the dragon in toilets (not injecting was the secret, she reckoned, to survive). The other fallen figures helped him rather than those who achieved enormous success (except for Pink Floyd's David Gilmour). During the entire period I knew him he struggled to get old associates to give him even a few hundred pounds to repair one of his two professional sewing machines, without which he could not work. They thought the price of a pair of shoes, the proceeds of a minor drawing, or a flash dinner was wasted on him, but he could not work without his machine. Under the sixties veneer of loveliness was extremely hard and cynical commercialism that hated failure. Some of the disdain for Ossie and his crowd came ironically from those cashing in on punk. Vivian Westwood and Malcolm McLaren produced a t-shirt in blue and red headed 'You're Gonna Wake up One Morning and Know What Side of the Bed You've Been Lying On.' Created in 1974, it features text devised by Maclaren with 'Hates 'listed on one side and 'Loves 'on the other. It had 'scum 'scrawled over a list of hates that included David Hockney (for 'Victorianism') and Ossie and many others of their milieu, including Chelita Secunda and Andy Warhol. Pauline is listed as 'Pauline Fordham halitosis'. Were it not for disliking the whole tasteless idea, these two would be on my list of hates. But his break-up with Nick Balaban depressed Ossie in his later years, not some maudlin pining for the sixties or his past life. Nick had been young when they met: as he grew older, he developed as an artist and even started his own fashion business selling his marvellous graphic t-shirt designs to Reiss, Top Man, BHS and boutiques. He needed the space and calm away from the turbulent wake Ossie left to find his voice.

"Ossie was devastated, and his world fell apart again. For two years, he stagnated in a state of total depression, always hoping Nick would return. For a time, he lived with me in an Islington council flat Nick and I had (Nick moved in with a new partner). They remained in contact, and gradually Ossie was reconciled to this second 'divorce'. Then, in 1991, Nick was diagnosed with AIDS, and depression descended again. Nick had also become disenchanted with fashion, selling his share of the business (Balaban and Nota Bene) he had startedn and returned to painting. Ossie encouraged him all he could, but the virus's effects became more and more debilitating. Finally, Nick was diagnosed with CMV, and blindness slowly descended. It is difficult to imagine the sense of helplessness this engenders if you have not experienced it. Nothing could change the diagnosis, and efforts to support him were thwarted by new infections and indignities. The experimental drugs were horrible to administer and caused as many problems as they aimed to solve. In the end, Nick needed love, and Ossie gave it to him.

"With Nick's death in 1994, Ossie slowly let go of the past. A tiny housing association flat began to be filled with new drawings and designs. Re-appraising his old work, he searched for a new silhouette for clothes. His genius for bias cut and complex material gained recognition working for Bella Freud and Ghost. With new boyfriend Diego, and the promise of financial backing from David Gilmore of Pink Floyd, it looked as if his star was rising again.

"Unfortunately, the mundane world came crashing into the enchanted one he was busily spinning around himself. After too much champagne at a fitting session, he impatiently nudged the car in front of him at a petrol station which unfortunately contained an off-duty police officer. A van load of reinforcements arrived. Ossie and Diego were arrested in a messy scene reminiscent of *Absolutely Fabulous*. Ossie was like Edina Monsoon and Patsy Stone rolled into one (the series is a disguised portrait of his circle, even down to the celebrity Buddhism that enormously helped Ossie find his feet). Probation for Ossie and community service for Diego followed. Stress of the court case and living together in Ossie's tiny flat with money worries took their toll. The relationship, disapproved of and unsupported by many of his straight friends and family, began to unravel. Ossie had used up his nine lives, and disaster followed when Diego, high on drugs and 'hearing voices from the Devil', smashed Ossie's skull with a flowerpot.

"The 'turbulent and ultimately tragic life of a flamboyant homosexual and drug user', as the *Daily Mail*'s Edward Verity put it, is not what I will remember of Ossie. Instead, I will remember a man who transformed the mundane world into an enchantment, who could make something from nothing, turning Sobranie cigarette packets into an intricate, mystically inspired mosaic inlay for his Buddhist shrine ('Look darling, isn't it fabulous'). It would be sad if this beautiful, chaotic, sometimes impossible man, who was talented and fun incarnate, who could cut a dress for Liz Taylor freehand whilst pissed at 2am, was remembered only as a broken butterfly of the sixties.

"I'll remember him draped in a cashmere throw, smoking a joint on the walk of the council flat in Islington and charming the neighbouring drug dealers. I remember arriving from college with Nick at Chelita's house to find Ossie in the kitchen. On asking what he'd been doing, he said, 'Oh, Pattie's here – we've been doing a fitting.' The next moment Pattie Boyd, wife of George Harrison and Eric Clapton (she is his 'Layla'), burst through the door wearing only the intricate armoured canvas corseted structure that held his strapless dresses in place. Her very ample breasts, like two large milk jellies and wobbling worryingly (you can tell I'm gay, can't you) in the structures Ossie had made for them were thrust into my 19-year-old face for assessment. I'll remember a Christmas Eve in which Francesca (Chessie) Thyssen-Bornemisza was thrown on the dirty floor of yet another loaned flat in Fulham strewn with tulips for a polaroid image later featured in the posthumous V&A exhibition. Afterwards, Ossie, hoping to gatecrash a David Sylvan party with her, tried to follow her fast car in his loaned and unlicensed bubble car with me as a passenger, pathetically slowly. He was forced to jump a red light and turned, almost hitting a police car. Parking as they turned to pursue, he said, 'Just walk away, darling, pretend nothing happened.' It didn't work, and after waiting for several hours for an (of course) over-the-limit 'Raymond 'Clark, I was forced, having missed the last trains, to call my father to collect Oscar and me. Ossie arrived two days later and charmed the pants off my parents.

"Like many exceptionally talented people, he could be hideously difficult, shouting at a waiter who vulgarly tried to shoo out party guests, referring to black me with the (very 1960s) 'spade ' or his anti-Semitic comments on 'jew boys'. This last stemmed from what he regarded as the deviousness of a Jewish business partner. Nick told me that he had been asked to sign a document in his usual scatty way as he hurried for a plane and this turned out to make him personally liable for his company's debts, placing his house and all his possessions in the hands of the taxman and creditors. He had also become violent as his marriage ended. The famous Hockney painting of 'Mr and Mrs Clark and Percy 'is a portrait of a three-way affair, and Ossie does not look comfortable in it. However, like the business deal, he allowed himself to sign up for what everyone thought was a good idea on paper. Everyone knew he was gay, but everyone encouraged a marriage of friends. When I first met him, I asked him about his sexuality, and he said, 'Oh darling, I'm just highly sexed.' Separated from Celia and living an entirely gay life, I thought it telling when he reported telling a doctor, 'I'm gay': several of the sixties people I knew, whilst swinging, were still highly affected, but the morality of their parents and the repercussions of being out in 'society 'made them conservative in acknowledging their sexuality publicly.

"I'll remember seeing the fashion show for Radley Gowns in the mid-eighties, where dresses with sleeves like seashells just stunned me. Grasping one particularly Baroque example, he said, 'Oh, you like that one – I cut it out at 2am this morning, isn't it devooo darling.' Or the sex party at Cynthia Payne's house – precisely like the film version in *Personal Services*. I'll also remember Nick saying, 'Do you want to see the Hockney painting?' and being taken upstairs to a cupboard in the attic. The unstretched canvas 'Life Painting for a Diploma 'was scrunched up and battered inside. Hockney had pulled it off the canvas after using it to fulfil the Royal College requirement, kept the drawing of a skeleton attached to it, and thrown the painting away. Thinking he might use the canvas in a dress, Ossie reclaimed it. Some years after seeing this sad remnant, a man approached Ossie at a party to say he had the skeleton drawing and wondered if they might come together. Reuniting the two, restoring it (miraculously), and bargaining with Hockney to recognise it, Ossie told me, resulted in no benefit to him at all. It eventually went to the Tate. Another of his cunning plans resulted in nothing to lift his status.

"When his friend Lady Henrietta Rous, who always tried to help him, edited *The Ossie Clark Diaries* (1998), I was horrified at the selection from his later years, picturing all the gloom but not the fun. It was even more upsetting that Nick was not pictured at all: expunged in favour of the 'real 'family and celebrities, it felt cruel. The same followed in various articles and books that resolutely focus on the 'heterosexual 'man (I could at least alter his Wikipedia page to balance things). I have mixed feelings now when I see his vintage outfits sell at hundreds of pounds, knowing he struggled to find buyers for a made-to-measure little black dress at £200 when he couldn't pay his rent. However, he continued to inspire some of us as he fluttered his bruised wings. In a world full of caterpillars, it takes balls to be a butterfly."

"Some people dream of having big swimming pools. With me it's closets."

Audrey Hepburn

My Thoughts

In 1998 a two-part documentary was made by the *South Bank Show*. The host, Melvyn Bragg, visited Ossie's flat, where the murder took place. Friends gave their thoughts on Ossie's decline and subsequent manslaughter, including his ex-wife Celia, Patrick Procter, and Marianne Faithfull. David Hockney and Ossie's sister Kay Clark gave their viewpoints on why they thought it happened. I want to add my point of view.

Ossie was an imperfect whizz kid who exploded into the fashion world like a Champagne Supernova bang in the middle of 1960s swinging London. In the 1950s, London was a dismal place for the day's teenagers, with its bombed, damaged buildings and pockmarked landscape. Ossie came along at the right time, along with many others, like Mary Quant and Biba; it became exciting, a place where everybody wanted to be and be seen.

He was one of the most, if not the most, influential fashion designers of the 60s/70s, bringing him into contact with all the leading lights of the day at the tender age of 25. Was it too soon? Did it all go to his head? Was he able to cope with being thrust into the limelight? He had no media training. Nothing prepared him for what lay ahead by 30, married with two children.

He was the toast of London: everybody wanted to know him and be seen wearing his clothes. It must have been so exciting for him. Although the myth about Ossie seems to be that he became a star overnight, he'd worked hard from the age of 13 when he attended art school in Warrington, Manchester, and for three years at the RCA in London. Hence, he did a good ten years of study before the world learned about his exceptional talent.

Ossie played a massive role in making London swing. What more recognition could a boy from Warrington need? The world wanted to copy his dresses; everything he did had style in mind as he tried to dress his friends. His friends wanted to spread the word of his genius. Who would have thought he could soar so high and then descend into the abyss with such alarming results that it almost beggars belief what happened to his life? David Bailey captured the mood of the 60s, and Ossie garbed the stars of the day in his illustrious way. Will we ever see such a decade again? It must have been an exciting time and a thrill to be a part of this kaleidoscope of colour. Ossie set trends, and people followed in their multitudes.

Chelsea and the King's Road conjure up pictures of glamour and sex, drugs, and rock and roll in our imagination. Who put these pictures in our minds, along with the writers of the day? Who hyped London to the maximum? None other than the boy from Warrington, who came to London with a dream and made it happen by sheer force of will. The Kings Road crystallised some of the best fashions to come out of London, celebrated in the fashion houses in New York and Paris.

Walking is always the best way to explore the Kings Road. Slip into a good pair of shoes, and you can still find some remnants of this hallowed road. Ditch your mobile phone and see what is going on down there. Take a walk back through time. The Kings Road is suited to be enjoyed when you are on foot. As you walk out of Sloane Square tube station, keep walking down the street till you reach the Chelsea Theatre at the World's End estate. You can soak up the atmosphere of this great part of London, housed in the Royal Borough of Kensington and Chelsea. It may not be what it once was. However, it is still worth your time to go along there and see yourself.

Learn about the art and literature that has sprung out of there, from the Sex Pistols to Oscar Wilde. But, of course, nothing is more enjoyable than checking out the shops and restaurants. I suggest going mid-week to miss the crowds that heave down there on Saturdays. Maybe Saturday is the only day you can manage because of work, but make sure you do it even if you are from outside of London and only coming in for the day. It will be tragic if you miss your itinerary of things to do in London. Wander along, and see some of the most expensive houses in London. Check out Oakley Street, where Oscar Wilde, Bob Marley and George Best lived, to name a few.

It is a breathtaking part of London. Wander down Oakley Street and see Cheyne Walk opposite the river Thames to check out the houses where Mick Jagger and Keith Richards lived; the King's Road and the World's End epitomised the counterculture of artistic influence and innovation of the 60s. And into the 70s, the World's End was home to the shop Sex, run by Vivienne Westwood and Malcolm McLaren, and the birthplace of punk rock and the anti-establishment that went on down there. You will not be disappointed. I guarantee you will have a lovely day checking out the area. It's an excellent place to live if you have the cash to splash out on a property. When I was a kid, people told me about London. It seemed such a daunting place when I arrived here in the 60s to visit my uncle, who lived in Islington. Nevertheless it excited my soul; I've never regretted moving here. But, of course, living in the Borough may not be everybody's cup of tea. If you try it for a few years, you may have a different point of view. I know I have. Anyway, I love it. I can see why Ossie spent the rest of his life here and raised a family.

Ossie inspired and made life exciting. It was never dull when he was around. What made him tick formed his character. Nobody else in the family would gain the recognition which came his way. His family raised him to be himself. They would have spoiled him. I'm sure he got used to being with women, with their love and encouragement from an early age. They built a boy who could hold his own with anybody. He learnt about life from them. With the significant success that came his way and the money and the glamour, we can blame nobody for his decline. He had bouts of depression and the taxman on his back. He must have felt the pressure. It would be so for anybody in that situation when he ended up skint. It's almost like it's better to have loved than never have loved. Ossie achieved something in his life. He would forever still have those memories, which many never did. Here we are still talking about him 24 years after his death. He was a kind and generous man. He may have been damaged, but we all have our dark sides. His played out in the public eye. He always had ambition. Even later, he believed he was on his way back. Where there is life, there is always hope. His friends in the neighbourhood where he lived on Penzance Place never said a bad word about him. He was an eccentric, granted, but nobody would notice this in London; it's normal around Portobello to see these characters. They bring a bit of light to the lives of people. I would rather sit in a pub talking to somebody like Ossie than sit with somebody with a plum in their mouth talking about stocks and shares; he lived a rich and varied life. He knew many people. He would have had so many exciting stories. He rose from a humble background and made something of his life. This is not your run-of-the-mill story or a work of fiction. This happened. He was a man with passion and a genuine love for life and his family. He tasted the fruit of success, watched his contemporaries rise, and was part of it; money doesn't make you happy.

Ossie left behind a legacy that will last forever; anybody interested in fashion mentions his name. This can never be taken away from him. We are all here briefly on this earth, but he matters. He made an impression in many ways. Royalty wore his creations. Yes, we cannot forget Celia. She was just as crucial to his success. As they say, behind every great man is a good woman. She is talented in her own right; her legacy speaks for itself. Celia doesn't want to talk about yesteryear. After all, they divorced 48 years ago, and Celia knows about Ossie. This woman bore him the children, but she has a life to deal with and doesn't want to dredge up the painful memories.

He carried himself like a rock star with an air of mystery. He wasn't pushy. He didn't ingratiate himself with people. His work spoke volumes. Nothing was too much for his family. It broke his heart to be separated from his children in the 70s. Still, he learned to live with it. The love for his boys never once diminished. I think they knew that this gave his sons strength also in later life to go out and do their own thing.

Who were the most influential people in his life, after his children and family, who helped him succeed? First would have to be his schoolteacher, Mr Roy Thomas from Beamont Technical School in Warrington. He fed Ossie with magazines, which sparked his interest in fashion at an early age, and encouraged him to go to art school, a turning point in the young Ossie's life. Celia Birtwell, for her common sense and textile genius, and the meeting and introduction of Alice Pollock as they all did remarkable things together. But, of course, Alice was introduced to Ossie through David Hockney.

Alice had a natural talent, and people noticed her when she spoke. The so-called swinging 60s came out of the art colleges. They were young, hip and influenced by the day's kids. Alice was in the background, toiling away; Ossie was out front, working alongside Celia. They each inspired the other. What an effective team they made. They were at the vanguard of the remarkable renaissance of British fashion and the psychedelic era of the 60s, along with Zandra Rhodes and Mary Quant.

And, of course, his friend and lover Nick Balaban, with whom he spent many happy years. When Ossie faded from the public eye, his life wasn't over. He was still a fantastic character, having fun and wheeling and dealing. People may not realise it can be fun chasing a dream or working on projects by ducking and diving, trying to conjure up plans to get back in the frame. It can still be satisfying even if you don't pull it off. So it wasn't the end of his world. Perhaps living like you and me, he still had the talent, the sharp mind, and the never say die attitude. He was a northerner, and they have tremendous fortitude and a down-to-earth sense of humour. Yes, sure, sometimes he sank into depression and maybe drank and took too many drugs than he should have. So many people cope this way when shit goes down. But he would come back. He had many interests, with his inquisitive brain and razor-sharp wit.

He lived more in his 54 years than most people could pack into several lives. This is not a depressing tale. It's the life story of a man who was a unique character we may never see again. We should feel privileged that he came along when he did. Nobody deserved the tragic ending that happened.

Many people in my hometown of Warrington have fond memories of when he returned to the town. He never boasted of his famous clients. Instead, he stayed close to his roots, and the warmth and love he received from his family gave him the strength to continue.

The friendship he formed with David Hockney went through many trials throughout 40 years, littered with great times and sad times. However, Hockney has memorialised Ossie forever with the masterpiece he gave Celia and Ossie as a wedding present. The Mr and Mrs Clark painting was the simple act of a friend. We must never forget this, no matter what happened between the two as the years rolled by. Ossie was emotional. His moods could swing. Perhaps he held a grudge against David, whose star soared and continues to soar. We shall never know. Does it matter all these years later? People are still talking about it.

Both left their stamp in their way. Ossie once said, "When Hockney creates a masterpiece, it ends up in the Tate, and when I do, it ends up in the bin six months later."

This is not strictly true after two major exhibitions and the exhibition held in his hometown of Warrington, which I attended with my son. Nevertheless, he will forever be remembered. He is still influencing young designers today. His clothes are still worn and coveted by Kate Moss, Naomi Campbell, and others.

If I had any anger in me for anybody in Ossie's life, I would direct it at the Italian Diego Cogolato, who viciously ended Ossie's life. Still, in his wisdom, the judge must have read the reports on Diego's mental health and decided how he must be punished. As unbelievable as it may seem to hand down such a short sentence, I can imagine the relief that escaped Diego's lips at such a lenient sentence. Did he hoodwink the judge, or was it so out of character that he would spend the rest of his life regretting his monstrous actions? I hope in remorse and contemplation he perhaps suffers late at night.

Celia did an outstanding job raising her boys and is still creating fashion over 55 years later. This is a mark of her creative genius. The family have survived and thrived together in a shared love of art, music and fashion.

I approached the family for interviews, and they threw a blanket of silence in my direction. I'm not sure if there is a divide between Ossie's and Celia's sides of the clan, but I don't blame them. Who wants to drag up the family business from years ago? There is no axe to grind. I did this project out of my fascination with Ossie. I realise I'm not going to please everybody, but I hope I've informed more people about Ossie. I suggest reading *The Ossie Clark Diaries* if you want to know further.

We should never forget Ossie for his talent and the joy he brought into people's lives. It has been an emotional journey for me authoring this book as I look back and think of those days when he arrived in the prime of his life. I was a starry-eyed schoolboy who knew nothing about the world. Never in a million years did I think how much the moment he stood on the stage would mean to me.

I was going through a crazy time when Ossie made a massive impression on my schoolboy brain. I wouldn't have believed I would author a book about him. That is strange when I stop and think about it. It shows how kids can be inspired by an adult, even for a moment in time.

Ossie's friends in the modelling world, especially those who bought his clothing, have good things to say about Ossie for his kindness and spirit. He helped where he could; if somebody were skint or getting married, he would let them off, wave them away, don't worry about payment, darling, you have a fun time.

He would have been 80 years old on the 9th of June 2022 and could have been still creating. So, in my small way, I would like to mark the life of a man who inspired me to go to university as I begin my journey at London's Birkbeck University in 2022 and do my degree. Ossie brought joy to many worldwide. I will raise a drink and salute you, sir.

I have learned that the real lesson we all must remember is that we are here one day and gone the next and live our lives the best way we can. Refusing to chase your dreams will give you an average life. Ossie made things happen. He didn't just get lucky. He put the time in to make it happen. The harder you work, the luckier you will get. It's that simple. It may be a cliché, but it's true.

A few months after Ossie's murder, newspapers revealed that a movie was to be made about Notting Hill starring the British actor, Hugh Grant. When the film was completed in 1999, it became one of the most sought-after places to live. And the film grossed the most money ever made by a UK film. Ossie, the last of the great bohemians in the area, must have spun in his grave. Property prices have risen, and astronomical amounts have driven out the working class—apart from the ones left behind in their council houses or housing association flats, including me. We are left to stare out on the street at the wealthy that inhabit the area and have no interest in Notting Hill's bohemian past. Still, it's a beautiful place to live and always worth visiting if you find yourself in this neighbourhood.

I also heard that in 2024, a film production company would make a documentary about Ossie's life. This has nothing to do with me, but it can only add to the legendary trailblazer's mystique, who left behind a body of work we can still admire today. Another book and film script is in the pipeline to depict Ossie's life. He more than deserves this.

Ossie regarded himself as an artist alongside Picasso and Matisse and as good as, if not better than, Yves St Laurent; his dresses were timeless and a work of art. I hope this film will be made about his extraordinary life.

"One hell of a fella"

About the Author

Tommy Kennedy IV, born in the North West of England. His early years were spent living in convents, caravans, and care homes around the UK.

He had a troubled childhood which resulted in him being sent to many Institutions, before finally leaving his hometown and heading to the bright lights of london.

After a few years in london, he spent over a decade travelling the world, living of his wits and not much else .

His love of music saw him running a bar and putting parties on in Thailand, where he came into contact with many musicians on his travels and made the fateful descion to head back to Notting hill, in 1999, setting up a music promotions company . He spent over 4 Years, homeless through drink and drugs and going bankrupt and losing his home .

He has spent the last 21 Years, living in London's Notting Hill, where he managed and promoted Bands. Including Managing Steve Dior, the legendary Punk Rock Singer who was hanging out with Sid Vicious when he died in New York .

Driving bands around the UK, and across Europe,he was kept very busy . He has been working for the last 16 years on the world famous Portobello Road, at the Mau Mau Bar, in Notting Hill, promoting gigs.

He has two children Sophie, and Tommy Jnr, the lights of his life. He is Currently working on his second book " Going Straight in Notting Hill Gate" about his release from the General Penitentiary in Jamaica, and working in the underground music scene in london, and turning his life around, which he Hopes to have finished sometime in 2020.
His philosophy on life, "find what you do best and share that knowledge to other people".

www.ingramcontent.com/pod-product-compliance
Lightning Source LLC
Chambersburg PA
CBHW070538170426
43200CB00011B/2463